DISCOVER
RUNES

UNDERSTANDING AND
USING THE
POWER OF RUNES

TONY WILLIS

Sterling Publishing Co., Inc.   New York

To T.J.E.
who taught me so much

Acknowledgements

I would like to express my thanks to Emily Peach for typing the manuscript
and offering invaluable support and encouragement throughout the project.

Library of Congress Cataloging-in-Publication Data Available

Willis, Tony.
  [Runic workbook]
  Discover runes : understanding and using the power of runes / Tony
Willis.
      p.   cm.
  Originally published: Runic workbook. Willingborough, Northamptonshire :
Aquarian Press ; New York, N.Y.: Distributed by Sterling Pub., 1986.
  Includes bibliographical references and index.
  ISBN 0-8069-0354-6
  1. Runes—Miscellanea.   I. Title.
[BF1623.R89W55   1993]
133.3'3—dc20   92–44470
                                                                    CIP

            1   3   5   7   9   10   8   6   4   2

          Published 1993 by Sterling Publishing Company, Inc.
              387 Park Avenue South, New York, N.Y. 10016
                  Originally published in Great Britain by
          The Aquarian Press under the title *The Runic Workbook*
                        © 1986 by Tony Willis
                  Distributed in Canada by Sterling Publishing
            % Canadian Manda Group, P.O. Box 920, Station U
                    Toronto, Ontario, Canada M8Z 5P9
                  Manufactured in the United States of America
                        All rights reserved

                    Sterling ISBN 0-8069-0354-6

CONTENTS

INTRODUCTION
How to use this book

The *Runic Workbook* is a basic introduction to the Runes and runic divination. The chapters should be worked through consecutively and the subject matter of each thoroughly mastered before moving on to the next. Naturally, everyone should work at his or her own pace, but the average person studying in their spare time will require about one week to assimilate each chapter.

The work is graded, which is a gentle way of saying that it gets progressively harder. It also means that the content of each chapter is built on the information contained in the chapters preceding it. For this reason it is not suggested that you simply open the book at some section that appeals to you and commence your studies there. This approach will only lead to confusion and, probably, a fair measure of disappointment into the bargain when you are finally forced to retrace your steps and start all over again at the beginning.

In each chapter there are certain facts that need to be memorized. In particular, you will need to remember the names and symbols of all the twenty-four Runes which make up the old Teutonic alphabet, the Elder Futhark, as given on page 25. These Runes are referred to by name throughout the text starting from Chapter 3 and it will considerably hamper your progress if you are not thoroughly conversant with them by the time you reach this point in the text. If you find that you have trouble remembering these names, or which name belongs to which symbol, you can mark page 25 with a bookmark or a paperclip for ease of reference. By far the most effective method of facilitating this learning process, however, is to equip yourself with a notebook and pen or pencil, and to keep these by you during your study period. You can then extract the relevant information from the chapter under review and write it up in the appropriate place in your notebook. It is a good idea, when dealing with the Elder Futhark, to allow one page per Rune. This regime should be adhered to even where your notes appear initially to be quite short as further information will be added in later chapters, and you will find that your ability to memorize is much improved by this process of summarizing and copying. Furthermore, you will finish up the proud possessor of a personalized handbook on the Runes, every word of which is both meaningful and evocative, and which will prove a powerful tool in your quest for inner wisdom.

The book is divided into two sections: Divination and Magic. This division is quite artificial, divination being merely a branch of magic. Most students however, make their initial forays into the occult while in search of practical guidance on how to live their lives more effectively and not during the course of some high-flown spiritual odyssey. For this reason, Part One deals primarily with divination while Part Two is more concerned with the subject of practical magic. The book has been laid out in this way so that those students who, for one reason or another, do not feel drawn to the more esoteric side of runic lore may, if they so wish, call a halt to their investigations at the end of Part One.

By deliberate choice there is no 'easy reference' list of page numbers where assessments of individual Runes may be found. A workbook is *not* to be used that way. Make notes of your own thoughts and feelings about the symbols and work from these. This is important if you are ever to kindle the spark of intuition within you. Besides, many of my minor comments about a Rune's meaning do not appear in the section given over to that Rune. Just check the index under ANSUR and you will see that I make 27 references to this Rune outside of the pages (48–50) on which I deal with it specifically.

In the section on divination, Chapters 3 to 7 take the Runes of the Elder Futhark five at a time and explain their meanings. These chapters also attempt to indicate how those meanings came to be associated with their respective Runes.

In both parts of the book, every chapter concludes with the description of a different type of runecast, or runic 'spread'. During the week allotted to the study of any particular chapter, the runecast from that chapter should be practised over and over again using all the Runes dealt with in the text to date. While you are still learning, it does not matter if you have no genuine question to put to the Runes. In fact, until you become more experienced in the art of divination, it is probably better to refrain from asking the Runes for their opinions on any subject that is really important to you. Above all, resist the temptation to find out about somebody else's private life for no higher motive than idle curiosity. As you will soon discover, the Runes have their own method of dealing with this type of enquiry.

As a novice seer, please do bear in mind that, since your training is partial, your answers too will be incomplete. Since you are not yet in a position to divine for other people, it is advisable that you *imagine* a client. Make this person totally imaginary. Do not use an absent acquaintance. You might say to yourself: 'I am consulted by a young woman. She wishes to know if she should marry her current boyfriend.' Or: 'A middle aged man wants to ask if this is a favourable time to make a career change.' Then lay out the Runes and interpret them to the best of your ability. Until you have learnt all twenty-four Runes of the Elder Futhark, your predictions will lack breadth and variety, especially when you are practising with only five or ten symbols. This is only to be expected. But you will find, as the weeks pass, that your readings soon flesh out and become more varied and profound.

Do not be in too much of a hurry to rush on to the next runecast in the book before you have familiarized yourself sufficiently with the earlier ones. It is a good idea to begin each week's divination exercise by using all the Runes whose meanings you have memorized to date — those in the chapter you are working on as well as those from the preceding chapters — and to practise *all* the runecasts you have already learnt. Then go on to try out the new runecast. If you neglect to follow this procedure, you could find that your progress is disconcertingly patchy, and a lot of students give up at this point under the impression that they have no aptitude for divination. The fault lies not in the system but in the fact that they have attempted to take in too much new material at one gulp. If you have been having great success using the runecast from Chapter 4 which uses only ten Runes, then it stands to reason that you put yourself back in the position of a novice when you start to learn the runecast from Chapter 5 together with the meanings of five new Runes. You can, however, ease yourself through this phase by following the above suggestion and using the fifteen Runes (ten old and five new) to interpret the two runecasts with which you are already familiar. When you have built up some confidence by doing this, you can then go on to the runecast from Chapter 5 without risking a trauma since you will now know how the five new Runes are likely to behave in divination.

While working on Part Two of the book, you should continue to devote a whole week to the work of each chapter since the runecasts in this section are more complex and generally require more practice than the simpler types dealt with in Part One. However, in Part Two there are no exercises in the making of runescripts and bindrunes. Every student's requirements will be different in this respect, but there is enough information in this section to enable anyone who has given a reasonable amount of time to the study of Part One to put these ancient and effective magical techniques into practice, and to do so without the fear that they may be inadvertently invoking negative energies into their lives or the lives of their friends. The system here presented is quite safe so long as one obeys the few simple rules.

With the purchase of this book, you are on your way to becoming a runic shaman. Resolve to be worthy of this ancient and noble calling. Pursue your studies with diligence and apply your knowledge with humility. The runic path is one which bestows upon its followers gladness of heart and a sense of joy in living, and I have yet to come across any student of the runic mysteries who regrets their decision to set their feet upon it.

PART ONE: DIVINATION

Chapter 1

AN INTRODUCTION TO

THE RUNES

Runes are the sacred symbols of the Teutonic races, and in the far past, a complete system of philosophy and magic was erected upon them. This system was handed down from shaman to pupil by word of mouth using the Runes themselves as mnemonics.

The word 'rune' comes from a root meaning both 'a secret' and 'to whisper', and obviously relates to a time before the invention of writing when all arcane knowledge was transmitted orally. However, the word also means 'a mystery', and when the early Christians wanted to translate the Gospels into the Germanic vernacular, they gave 'runa' exactly that significance in Matthew 4, ii: 'the mystery of the Kingdom of God'. But a mystery is not just something held secret by one group of people from another; it can be something which transcends mere intelligence, something which can be understood or experienced but which cannot be taught for it cannot be put into words.

The idea that runic lore had to be passed on by word of mouth withstood the invention of writing, and even the creation of a runic alphabet could not induce the runemasters of old to produce a thesis on runic knowledge. All that survives along these lines is a handful of poems taking the Runes as their theme: the Scandinavian and Anglo-Saxon 'Runic Poems' and the 'Husband's Message', with its beautiful example of runescript magic. None of these poems, however, explain the method for using the Runes, or the rationale behind them, so that the uninitiated are none the wiser on that score for having read them. These alphabet-poems were all written well into the Christian era when a fusion of the native religion with the newer faith had done much to invalidate the original beliefs. I have come across people attempting to use these alphabet-poems to interpret the Runes in divination, but it is not a method I would recommend unless one has a reasonably good grounding in runelore to fall back on, for the poems are full of deliberate errors and conundrums — of which the Anglo-Saxons and the Teutonic races generally were very fond. For example, SIGEL, the symbol for the letter S in the runic alphabet and which means 'the sun', is treated in the 'Anglo-Saxon

Rune Poem' as if its name were SEGEL, meaning 'a sail'.

Like the Celts, with whom they had much in common, the Teutons preferred to rely mainly on memory for the safe transmission of their secret wisdom. Just as the Bards and Druids learned by heart the teachings of their predecessors, so the runic magician was expected to memorize the meanings and uses of all the various Runes. In this way, the tradition has been handed down to the present time almost intact.

It is wrong to assume (as many people do) that runic knowledge ever died out. Despite appearances to the contrary, runelore has been preserved in the most unlikely places and in the most unexpected ways. This was made necessary by the persecution directed against runic magicians — and the history of the decline of runic divination and magic is also the history of the increasing penalties exacted for their open practice. You will often read in books about the Runes that the runic magicians of Iceland 'died-out' in the seventeenth century. What actually happened was that in 1639 the Church officially banned the use of the Runes, and in consequence no one thereafter would admit to having anything to do with them. When knowledge is outlawed, however, it does not vanish away as if it had never been, it merely goes underground; and this is what happened with the Runes. Their wisdom continued to be passed on in secret (usually from father to son, or mother to daughter) so that not only did it survive, but it remained a living, growing tradition.

It was not hard for the runic initiates to adapt to the new conditions imposed upon them by the Christian Church, for they were not priests in any conventional sense. Unlike the pagan faiths common to Western and Southern Europe which were hierarchic and hierophantic in organization, the Germanic/Norse tradition is essentially shamanistic. The runic magician usually worked alone, not in a group; and there were no recognized grades — though obviously some initiates were better magicians than others. (Nevertheless, we can be sure there were no incompetents among their number, for in those days a magician was rewarded solely on results!) Some of these runic magicians were settled in one place, attending to the needs of the villages around them, but others travelled about the countryside taking work where it was offered. There was no sexual discrimination: both men and women were eligible to become shaman.

At the time the Teutonic races come to the notice of historians, they were passing through a period of conquest and colonization, and most of the men were preoccupied with the arts of war. This left the occult field open to the women, and there are many references in Norse literature associating runelore with women. The clearest description we have of a runic practitioner is of a female shaman. It comes from the *Saga of Erik the Red*, and was written in the thirteenth century:

She wore a cloak set with stones along the hem. Around her neck and covering her head, she wore a hood lined with white catskins. In one hand she carried a staff with a knob on the end, and at her belt, holding together her long dress, hung a charm pouch. She wore calfskin shoes and catskin mittens to cover her hands at all times.

There is other documentary evidence which shows that the Runes were used for both magic and divination. The method of divination was similar to the drawing of lots. For all ancient peoples the casting of lots was a method of augury: how the lot fell, or whichever lot came to hand being considered to represent the will of the god or gods invoked to preside over the ceremony. Tacitus, in his *Germania*, Chapter 10, describes the Teutonic method of consulting the Runes:

> To divination and the casting of lots they pay more attention than any other people. Their method of casting lots is a simple one: they cut a branch from a fruit-bearing tree and divide it into small pieces which they mark with certain distinctive signs and scatter at random onto a white cloth. Then the priest of the community, if the lots are consulted publicly, or the father of the family, if it is done privately, after invoking the gods with eyes raised to heaven, picks up three pieces, one at a time, and interprets them according to the signs previously marked upon them.

This is exactly the traditional method of runic divination as described in Chapter 3, the one in common use until the time of the Industrial Revolution in those areas of Great Britain that had been settled by the Angles, Jutes, and Saxons, or by the Danes and Vikings. It is a method still much favoured by runic diviners, and comes down to us in unbroken transmission from a time earlier even than Tactitus.

By going underground, the runic system survived as an unpublished, and unpublicized magico-mystical tradition in all the Anglo-Saxon, Germanic and Scandinavian countries — and this includes the United States which took in immigrants in large numbers from all those areas. At the end of the nineteenth century, the teaching first began to be written down in a formulated and coherent fashion. The bulk of this work was done by German and Austrian occultists, sometimes using material that had been transmitted orally, but more usually working via the method of analeptic recall.

Unfortunately, the defeat of Germany at the end of the First World War led certain German occultists to vaunt the Runes as significators of national identity — part of the ethnic inheritance of the Master Race. This is a perversion of the philosophy that lies behind the runic mysteries, which teaches that the secrets of the Runes are open to anyone, irrespective of sex, race, or colour. No one, after all, would suggest that the I Ching can only be used by the Chinese; that only the Arab races can ever become proficient in Geomancy, or that the Tarot can be expected to work only in the hands of the linear descendants of the Gypsies or the Ancient Egyptians (both of which races have been hailed as the 'inventors' of the Tarot by various savants). The truth of the matter is that all these techniques move very easily from one geographical location to another, and between one race and another, if only they are passed on by enlightened and sympathetic explicators.

In the event, the appropriation of the Runes by the higher echelons of the Nazi party did the advancement of runic lore no good at all in the years following the Second World War. Hitler used the old Aryan symbol of the Sun-Wheel, the Swastika, as the emblem of Nazism; Himmler had the insignia of the notorious S.S. expressed in Runes (a fact that escaped most people's attention at the time, and continues to do so), and after the collapse of the Nazi war machine the Allies very naturally wanted nothing at all to do with Runes: neither did the German nation itself, busily repudiating the Nazis and all their works and anxious to avoid guilt by association in any form. The Runes were consequently consigned to the occult wilderness. Only one article on Runes was published in the United Kingdom between the middle 'forties and the early 'seventies, and that article (written in the late 'fifties) dealt with an aspect of the runic tradition that was absolutely untainted by Nazi associations.

Not until the Second World War had faded from memory and a new generation who had never experienced it had grown to adulthood did the Runes begin to enjoy a renaissance. This revival of interest started in a small way — as such revivals always do. Researchers began to study the books of the German authors who had been writing at the turn of the century and, simultaneously, the runic initiates of Scandinavia, Germany, Great Britain and America began to disseminate information on divination by the Runes, which is the most accessible — and thus the most popular — aspect of runic lore.

During this period, the Runes and runic philosophy were being impressed upon the consciousness of the post-war world, particularly among the English-speaking peoples, through the surprising agency of J.R.R. Tolkien. In *The Lord of the Rings*, the Dwarves are said to use the Runes for communications, and this runic alphabet is explained in that part of the Appendix to *The Lord of the Rings* which deals with writing in Middle Earth.

Tolkien was a professor of Anglo-Saxon, and the whole work (*The Hobbit* and the three books of *The Lord of the Rings*) is shot through with glimpses of Teutonic Mythology.

In occult circles, however, it was not until the early 'eighties, when interest in the Runes had reached a high pitch, that the guardians of the runic tradition gave the order for a further release of information — this time of a deeper and more esoteric nature. This is where we stand today, on the brink of a new dawn of runic instruction. Not only is the ancient wisdom now being revealed more openly than ever before, it has also become easier for dedicated seekers to penetrate the more recondite and abtruse aspects of runic lore. Additionally, and for those who prefer group workings, there are **Odinic Lodges**, as the runic Mystery Schools are called, operating all over Northern Europe, North America, and even Australia.

Symbols Runes and Alphabet Runes

For our purposes, we may consider that Runes divide into two basic types. The first type consists of symbolic pictures, some of which are easy to interpret and

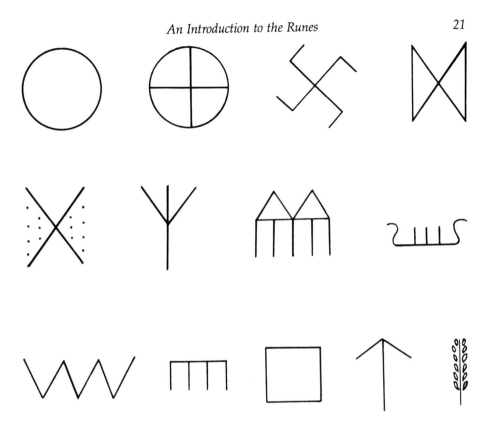

Figure 1: Symbol Runes

some of which are more obscure. Quite logically, this type of Rune is called a Symbol Rune, and Figure 1 shows some examples of these.

The reason why many of these Symbol Runes are difficult for the modern mind to comprehend is that the early Teutons never went in much for realism in art, but always retained a formal, non-representational style right down to the time of the Vikings. Figure 2 has been copied from a carving on an axe-head and is meant to depict a bearded face. It is, in fact, a stylized portrait of the god Thor, and once you know what it is, you have no difficulty in recognizing it. A casual observer, however, might be forgiven for mistaking it for mere ornamentation, and this is the problem the twentieth-century mind is faced with when attempting to decipher Symbol Runes.

We must suppose that, because the symbols conformed to certain recognizable conventions, Symbol Runes were perfectly understandable to the peoples among whom they were current. The key to this symbolism being lost, however, modern scholarship is not always in a position to tell what a particular symbol is meant to convey. Some Symbol Runes have had their meanings preserved in one way or another and we can, therefore, make a

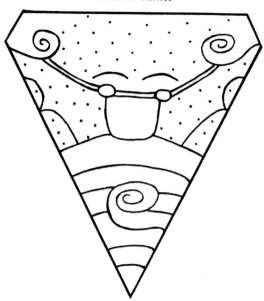

Figure 2: Stylized Portrait of Thor

guess as to their pictorial significance. Figure 3, for example, is a protective sign. As such, it could represent a palm and outstretched fingers (which is a well-known avertive sign in all cultures); or the face and horns of an elk or reindeer, prime sacrificial beast of the Northern Tribes (all sacrifices being originally intended to secure the protection of the gods); or it could indicate the Teutonic invoking stance as mentioned by Tacitus: upright, with the arms raised above the head.

The second type of Rune is the Alphabet Rune. Alphabet Runes are glyphs used to represent sounds in the ancient Germanic language in the same way that our present alphabet is used to represent the vowels and consonants of modern speech — but we must never lose sight of the fact that Alphabet Runes are nothing more than a modified form of Symbol Rune: all Alphabet Runes are Symbols Runes — but not all Symbol Runes are Alphabet Runes.

The word 'alphabet' derives from the first two letters of the Greek alphabet — alpha and beta — and this seems to have been the usual method of naming alphabetic sequences among primitive peoples. Anyone who has read Robert Graves' *The White Goddess* will know that this was the way in which the Celts named their alphabets, the Beth-Luis-Nion and the Boible-Loth. Similarly the runic alphabets are named after their first six letters which, by a happy coincidence, spell out the word FUTHARK. All versions of the runic alphabet commence with these same six letters, and so all runic alphabets are called Futharks.

There are three main Futharks: the Elder or Common Futhark; the Younger (or German) Futhark, and the Anglo-Saxon Futhark. The Elder Futhark, as its name suggests, was the prototype from which the Younger and Anglo-Saxon Futharks were later adapted. In this book, we will be dealing mainly with the Elder Futhark and the twenty-four glyphs of which it is comprised, but there is also a section on the Anglo-Saxon Futhark.

All three of these Futharks were expressions of the same magical/divinatory system adapted to the various tribal, political and climatic conditions in which the different divisions of the Germanic races developed. The Anglo-Saxons, for instance, were encouraged to expand the traditional Futhark, first to twenty-eight letters, and later to thirty-three letters, because of the linguistic changes that occurred once the Angles, Jutes and Saxons had settled in Britain. Removed from any kind of regular intercourse with their fellow Teutons, their dialect soon became rich in dipthongs, and — gradually — dipthongs began to outnumber vowels, and the Anglo-Saxon shaman provided new symbols to represent the new sounds. These symbols were then tagged on to the end of the existing alphabet; but the pattern of the Elder Futhark continued to influence the Anglo-Saxon method of runic divination. Despite the expansion of their Futhark, the Anglo-Saxons continued to use only twenty-four Runes for the purposes of divination, and so strong was their religious conservatism that in one instance only did a 'modern' Rune succeed in usurping the place of a traditional, continental one.

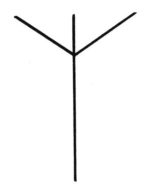

Figure 3:   A Protective Sign

A few Alphabet Runes were 'invented' or created at the time the Elder Futhark was assembled, but most of them were adapted from the already existing store of Symbol Runes. Figure 3, which we have already examined, is a good example of this process. It is only due to the fact that this Rune entered the Elder Futhark that scholars are able to be so certain as to its meaning, though we can now only guess at the physical object it was meant to represent.

Every Rune in the Elder Futhark is named after an object, an animal, an emotion, or — occasionally — a god. This is no more than we should expect, since Alphabet Runes were adapted from Symbol Runes. It is quite natural that Symbol Runes would be named after the thing they were intended to

Discover Runes

symbolize. It is possible that the Symbol Runes that were finally selected to make up the Elder Futhark were chosen because the initial letters of their names were the same as the letters they were needed to denote. Thus the Symbol Rune for 'hail', whose name was HAGALL, was co-opted — if this theory is correct — as the Alphabet Rune for the aspirate 'H'.

The runic names of all three Futharks follow this pattern. The one exception to this rule is the Rune ING. This Rune represents the sound 'ng', usually shown by linguists as ᛝ . In this case, 'ng' is incorporated in the name of the Alphabet Rune, but not as the first letter — or in this case, sound — in that name. This is because, though the gutteral 'ng' is common in the primitive Germanic language, this language contains no words that commence with that sound. The next best solution, therefore, was to choose a short name, preferably containing a single syllable, which emphasized the required sound — and this would seem to be precisely what the Teutonic shaman did.

Figure 4 shows the twenty-four letters of the Elder Futhark with their letter names in the Yorkshire-Viking dialect in which I was taught them. These are the names that will be used throughout the book, and I suggest you take a few minutes to familiarize yourself with them.

There is another set of names which have attained wide popularity among runic students. In it the Rune I call WYNN is known as *wunjo*, LAGU is *laguz*, etc. I am not happy with these names. For one thing, we are not certain that they were ever used by the Teutons or Indo-Europeans. They are the invention of a branch of linguistics which attempts to ascertain what languages sounded like in the dim and distant past. The names I was taught, on the other hand, are part of a living tradition. They can be found, with slight variations, in Elliot and Page (*see* Bibliography) and Koch (*The Book of Signs*, Dover Publications Inc., New York). Pronunciation is a matter of personal preference, naturally, but to me the names given here ring true; they have depth, meaning, resonance. In short, they are, for me, tremendously evocative tools which greatly augment my ability to divine.

Historians complain that the runic alphabet developed quite late in comparison with the alphabets of other cultures. There is some controversy as to exactly when the Elder Futhark came into being, but it is thought to have occurred at some period between 200 BC and AD 200. By that time, the Cretans, Phoenicians, Greeks, Etruscans and Romans had already been using alphabetic writing for several centuries — not just for recording mundane or bureaucratic minutiae but to compose sophisticated poetry and intelligent scientific treatises. Because of the advanced state of literacy among other cultures, scholars have tended to look down on the Runes as unworthy of interest. They are dismissed as being a cheap imitation of the other alphabets with which the Germanic tribes inevitably came into contact in the early years of the Christian era.

This theory has led many scholars to regard the Runes as having no value other than for the straightforward transliteration of inscriptions on runic monuments or runic artifacts. Yet the evidence bequeathed to us by history — from Tactitus to the Venerable Bede — suggests the exact opposite: that Alphabet Runes never relinquished their function as Symbol Runes. In magical inscriptions, Alphabet

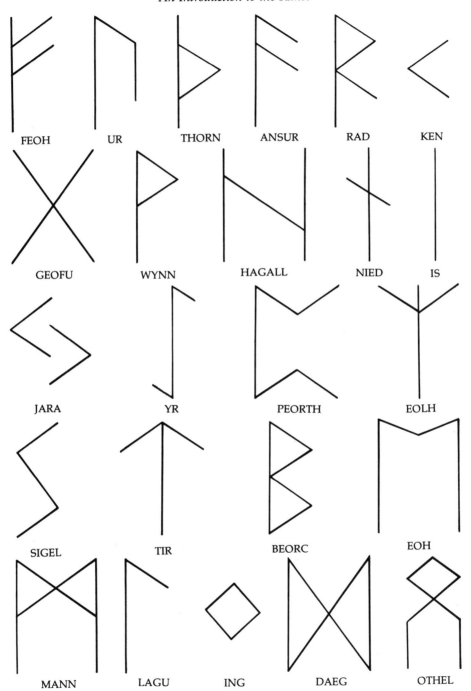

Figure 4: The Elder Futhark

Runes are always employed in this way, and even in secular scripts an Alphabet Rune would frequently be used in a symbolic way, i.e. *as if it represented not a sound, but a thing in itself*. In one Anglo-Saxon Runic Poem, for example, each stanza commences with a single Rune which must be read *as a symbol* in order to extract the full sense of what the poet is saying. Thus, the poem tells us that ᚦ (the Rune used to represent the sound 'th', but which means 'a thorn') is 'very sharp to every man'. It would be simply perverse to read this as ' "th" is very sharp' — so much so that no scholar cares to do so.

J.M. Kemble admits in his *Anglo-Saxon Runes* (Andrew Publishing Company, 1976): 'There are inscriptions in Anglo-Saxon Runes, but in no Teutonic language.' And he continues in a footnote: 'There are several other runic lines which can hardly be looked upon as anything but the idle amusement of transcribers, some of them being apparently mere collections of consonants without vowels, and vowels without consonants.' This is to miss the point. The reason non-linguistic groupings of Runes could be made was that Alphabet Runes were derived from Symbol Runes and, for magical purposes, continued to hold that significance — and still do, as we shall see in Chapters 9 and 10.

Chapter 2

FIRST STEPS IN
DIVINATION

Choosing Your Rune Set

The first Runes were not written on paper, but engraved on stone or carved on bark, and from this they obtained their distinctive angular shape. If you have ever attempted to inscribe your initials on the bark of a tree, you will know that the process is made easier by reducing the letters to a series of straight lines. The Teutonic shaman made the same discovery over two thousand years ago; and because the most primitive Alphabet Runes were angular, the most effective rune-sets seem to be those which retain this original peculiarity — even where the medium no longer necessitates it. Figure 4 shows the Elder Futhark, the runic alphabet with which we shall be dealing most closely in these pages, drawn in the angular mode.

Some rune-sets do not retain this linear convention, being based on later developments of the runic alphabet — particularly those derived from Anglo-Saxon Britain which had begun to develop a cursive script before runic writing was completely ousted by the Latin alphabet favoured by the clerics of the day — and I shall be giving these curvilinear alternatives when we come to look at each Rune individually in Chapters 3 to 7, but personally I prefer an angular set with no curved lines at all, these being more in the spirit of the primitive, carved Runes. Most rune-sets on sale today, however, contain at least one cursive Rune, and so it may be that you will have to examine one or two of the Runes in your chosen set in order to identify them properly.

Your rune-set should be made out of some natural substance, one either drawn from the earth (like clay) or produced by the earth (like wood). Plastic is not recommended because it is out of harmony with the inner vibrations of the runic symbols, which are earthy and practical, while plastic is a derivative of oil and therefore vibrates to the powers of Neptune which can be deceptive and illusionary if not handled with care.

Additionally, there are at least two sets of Rune Cards on the market, one specifically designed to accompany this book. If you find clay or wood too cumbersome, you might feel more at home using a pack of these.

At the end of this book is a list of suppliers, and you should be able to obtain a set of Runes from any of these. However, it has always been an occult maxim that the magician or diviner should forge his or her own magical tools; the reasoning behind this being that whatever we make ourselves absorbs something of our own essence in the process, and because of the affinity between us and it, will always deal with us truly. The most accurate rune-set, therefore, is the one you make yourself. This can be modelled from clay, burnt in poker-work onto small rectangles of wood, or drawn in felt-tipped pen onto blank playing cards.

If you decide to colour your Runes, or want to buy a coloured set, *all* the Runes in the set should be painted or dyed in one of the traditional colours. These are: red for energy (most effective for the male shaman); green for growth (often chosen by the female shaman or by followers of the Goddess); or blue — the colour sacred to Odin, tutelary deity of runic knowledge.

Carrying Pouch and Rune Cloth

Besides the Runes themselves you will require two other items before you are ready to commence your training as a runic diviner. The first of these is a small bag in which to carry your Runes. This makes it easier to transport the Runes from place to place, and also ensures against loss or misplacement of single Runes. Many rune-sets come complete with a carrying pouch, but if yours does not, you can easily buy or make one. Like the Runes themselves, it should be made of some natural material, such as wool, cotton, velvet or linen rather than a synthetic fabric or one that is a mixture of natural and manmade fibres. Often, bags of this type are on sale at the many occult festivals which go on all over the country throughout the year, or they can be purchased from an occult supplier.

In order to 'power up' the Runes, the Teutonic shaman always used to carry their rune pouches on them, usually tied to their waists like the female shaman described in the previous chapter. You can achieve much the same results by sleeping with your pouch under your pillow, or (by day) tucking the pouch under your sweater while you watch T.V. or read a book. In the latter case, the best place to position the pouch is on the stomach just below the navel, or over the solar plexus — the small depression about the size of a fifty-pence piece half way between the navel and the throat. Both of these are power points in the body, and contact with them will allow the Runes to pick up and attune themselves to your own personal vibratory rate. The difference made to the accuracy of one's divination by this means is quite amazing. Very often the progress made after two or three lessons is due as much to the student's constant handling of the Runes as to their increased familiarity with the symbols. This is something you will probably notice for yourself as you progress through Chapters 3 to 7 of this book.

The second item you will require is a plain white cloth on which to lay out your Runes. This is a traditional piece of equipment, as may be surmised from

Tacitus's remarks on Teutonic divination given in the previous chapter. It may seem a superfluous requirement, but it fulfils a very necessary function. The method of shuffling Runes is to swirl them around using the flat of your hand, and if you do this on an unprotected table-top you will inevitably score the veneer. Additionally, some diviners (myself included) prefer to use the ground as a working surface (being an 'earthy' divinatory system, the Runes seem to work better the closer they are to Mother Earth) and if you take up this practice and fail to use a cloth, you will soon find that your Runes become dirty and greasy — no matter how clean you think your carpets are. And for working in the open air, some sort of protection is a must.

In my experience, it is not absolutely essential that the cloth is white, but it is important that it is of a *single* colour. The cloth is intended to provide the Runes with a neutral background, and should not distract the diviner's attention from them in any way. For this reason, it is best to avoid vibrant colours and jazzy patterns, as well as fringes and embroidered symbols. If you are at all undecided as to colour or material, choose a white linen table-napkin. This makes an excellent work surface, is exactly the right size, and is sanctioned by tradition and usage.

Casting the Runes
Runic divination is sometimes referred to as 'casting the Runes'; and with the more primitive method, which uses nine Symbol Runes etched on stones, the Runes are indeed 'cast' or tossed, either directly onto the ground or onto the diviner's cloth. Racial memories of this practice have influenced the language of runic divination, in spite of the fact that Alphabet Runes are not generally 'cast'. In runic parlance a 'runecast' is the equivalent of a Tarot Reader's 'spread', that is to say, it is the method or order in which the symbols are laid out prior to interpretation.

Every runecast has its own distinctive pattern; but the preliminary preparations and the way in which individual Runes are selected to make up that pattern remain the same in every case.

1.   Lay out your plain cloth on the table or patch of floor you intend to use as your work surface. Tip the Runes from their carrying pouch onto the cloth.

In the early stages of your studies, you will only be working with those Runes whose associations and attributions you have already learned. Where this is the case, you should separate the Runes you are as yet unfamiliar with from those you will be using for your divination practice and put them back in the pouch.

When working with all twenty-five Runes of the Elder Futhark, you should lay them out in their alphabetic sequence in three rows of eight with the Blank Rune a little apart from the rest — either above, or below, the others. This is simply to ensure that all the Runes are accounted for, and that none are left in the pouch or have otherwise gone astray.

At this point, some diviners make a short, silent, invocation to one of the Guardians of the Runes — Odin or Freyja — to ask that the Runes might give a clear and accurate answer to their question. You may prefer to call upon some god or force (such as the Higher Self) with which you are more familiar — or you may prefer to disassociate yourself from this facet of runic practice entirely. Your own personal belief system will dictate your decision here, and it is not for me to try to influence you in any way. I will say, however, in the interests of religious and philosophical tolerance, that *all* these methods seem to work *as long as the diviner truly believes in them.*

2.   Turn all the Runes you are using face downwards, and swirl them around in a clockwise direction with the palm of your right hand. Keep this up until you can no longer remember where any of the Runes in the group are. This is the runic method of 'shuffling'.

It is not of world-shattering importance that you use your right hand for swirling or shuffling the Runes: it is just that it is easier for a right-handed person to make a circle with their right hand in a clockwise direction. A left-handed person may, of course, use their left hand if they find it more convenient.

Alternatively, you may have been trained in the school of thought that states that the right hand of a right-handed person is active and conscious, while the left hand is passive and represents the subconscious, and that for a left-handed person, the opposite is the case. If you have, you might want to employ your 'subconscious hand' as an extension of your subconscious mind.

It is not important, either, that the Runes be swirled in a clockwise direction — though most occultists will insist on doing it this way because of the strong association in European folklore of clockwise motion with the 'good' magic of blessing and increase, and of anti-clockwise motion with the 'evil' magic of cursing and decrease. If you adhere to this belief (and the vast majority of people do, even outside the world of occultism) then it is only logical that you should swirl the Runes widdershins (anti-clockwise) when asking a question to do with decrease, banishing, or the ending of something. Therefore, enquiries such as 'Will I be able to give up smoking?' or 'Should I divorce my spouse?' should be accompanied by an anti-clockwise swirl.

3.   Select the Runes required to form your runecast one at a time, and place them before you — face down — according to the relevant diagram in the text.

You will find that if you move your hand, palm downwards, over the backs of the Runes about half an inch above their surfaces, some will seem more attractive or appealing to your subconscious mind than others, and thus you will choose those. Your conscious mind is unable to make a choice of this kind, and you can be sure that you have slipped back into a conscious mode of thought if you find yourself dithering between two exactly similar backs. Should this occur, you are advised to choose neither of the two Runes concerned, but to return your mind to subconscious mode and recommence running your hand over the backs of the remaining Runes instead. Then make your selection. You will more than likely find yourself choosing one of the Runes that you were initially undecided about — and what has probably happened is that the subconscious mind, about to make its selection, has been interrupted by the conscious mind saying: 'Hey! What do you want to choose that one for? Why not the one next to it? What's the difference?' When your mind dithers between two Runes, they are generally lying adjacent to one another, and to the conscious mind, of course, there is no difference between two face-down Runes as all the backs are (or should be!) exactly alike. Thus, the conscious mind, which works through logic, has no criteria by which to make its decision. The subconscious mind, however, senses (or feels) a difference; and this is why I describe the business of selection in emotional terms like 'attraction' or 'appeal'. The subconscious mind makes its choice instinctively and unerringly.

It is irrelevant whether Runes are laid out from right to left or from left to right. When used for communication, Runes could be written in either direction, but because the modern convention is to write from left to right, the Runes are generally laid out in this direction too. It is only important, in those runecasts where each position has a meaning, that the order in which the Runes are laid out be remembered so that there can be no confusion when it comes to interpretation. For this reason, it is better to be consistent in your practice than to set out the Runes for each divination just as the mood takes you.

4.   Turn over the Runes, and interpret them.

Always turn over the Runes as if they were pages in a book so that you do not alter the direction in which they are facing. Thus, upright Runes will remain upright, and reversed Runes will remain reversed.

It is good practice to turn the Runes over position by position, and to interpret the Rune or pair of Runes thus uncovered before looking to the Rune in the next position. Some people, however, prefer to turn over all the Runes in the cast right at the very beginning so that they can get a holistic view of the situation.

Once again, it is of no real importance which of these alternatives you choose. What is important is that you should adopt one set method of doing things *and stick to it*. The object here is to build up a routine and to follow it through without variation or deviation. This diminishes the amount of work the conscious mind has to do and thus enables you to throw your conscious mind into neutral, as it were. The conscious mind then no longer has to worry about 'What do I do next?', because a familiar routine takes over, and absolves it of all decisions. This is the rationale behind all ritual, whether it is employed in the orthodox worship of the church or in the rather more unorthodox observances of magicians and shaman: it encourages a quiescent conscious mind so that the subconsious may rise up and seek contact with the Divine. Divination — as the name suggests — has the same end in view.

If you have no previous training with a School, Lodge or Tradition, and have picked up no teaching or set of beliefs through your study of occult literature, then it is probably better that you follow the instructions given here to the letter. You may rest assured that all the directions are based upon solid precepts even where you are not able immediately to perceive what those precepts may be. As your studies in other areas of occultism broaden your understanding, however, you may wish to make alterations to the system outlined above. This is perfectly admissible — in fact, it is essential. It is more important to do something because you understand it and believe in it than to do it because you have been told that it is the right thing to do — no matter how revered or elevated your instructor may be! — and are following those instructions blindly. I have given you reasons why the right hand is the preferred hand to swirl the Runes with for right-handed people, and why the swirl is made in a clockwise direction. And there are reasons for *every* instruction given. Sometimes the reason is practical — as with the white cloth and the use of the right hand for swirling. Sometimes it is mystical or philosophical — as with the reason for favouring a clockwise motion for the swirling over an anti-clockwise one. Either way, however, there always is a reason, and it is always a good one.

Never make a change to the instructions given here simply for the sake of it. If you have a reason for making an alteration that seems valid to your conscious mind, then by all means implement it, because the more your conscious mind accepts the logic of what you are doing the easier it is to lull it into abeyance — and that, after all, is the object of the exercise.

The same applies, of course, if you already have a grounding in occult science: you are at liberty to make any *informed* alterations necessary to bring these instructions into line with your beliefs.

Runic Divination
Runic divination has affinities with all the other methods of prediction that rely on the fortuitous allocation or selection of symbols to stimulate the seer's latent clairvoyance into activity. This type of divination is called *fluidic* or *mutable*. Thus, runic divination has similarities with divination by the Tarot, Geomancy, Dice Throwing, the I Ching and Horary Astrology; but not with divination by Palmistry, Phrenology or Natal Astrology where the symbols are fixed and unchanging from diviner to diviner.

Every human being possesses a degree of clairvoyant ability, though in the majority of people it is supressed. All forms of fluidic divination are intended to awaken the diviner's natural psychism, to act as a bridge between the rational thought processes of the conscious mind and the intuitive mode of mentation employed by the subconscious mind. Here is how the runic system sets about building that bridge.

Each Rune has a series of concepts associated with it. Almost invariably, these concepts are expressed as symbols or pictures. This is because the subconscious mind thinks in pictures rather than in words. Any series of closely allied concepts is called an 'association chain' or a 'symbol string'. Each picture in an association chain fits together with the preceding and succeeding pictures in an entirely logical way — though this logic may employ the methodology of lateral, as opposed to sequential, thinking, for lateral thinking is the mode of thought most congenial to the subconscious mind.

The use of an association chain makes the feat of memory easier and, in reality, the Runes are a system of mnemonics. Thus, because each symbol in a chain is associated with the next symbol in the sequence (in however tenuous a manner), the effort required to memorize all the correspondences is considerably less than one might imagine.

For instance, the first symbol in the Elder Futhark is the Rune FEOH, which means 'cattle'. Its main association is with wealth, for in the days when the Alphabet Runes were first assembled, a man's wealth was determined by the size of his herds, and an increase in livestock meant an increase of substance. But an increase in livestock is also connected with the idea of fertility or fertilization, the mating of cow with bull; so, by analogy, this Rune can also indicate a measure of sexual fulfilment, even among humans. Finally, from the cow we obtain leather, meat and milk and its derivatives, butter and cheese, so that FEOH also embraces the concept 'to be nourished', 'to be provided for'.

Although each Rune represents a multitude of ideas, no matter how diverse or mutually exclusive these ideas might appear to be at first sight, there is always a definite connection between them. Once this connection is found, a large number of related concepts can be drawn up into the conscious mind with comparative ease, as if they were all strung together like beads on a necklace.

Psychoanalysis makes use of this habit of subconscious mentation when it asks a patient to do a word association test ('What does this word remind you of?'), or an ink-blot test ('What does this shape remind you of?'). Occultists, too, have long understood this property of the subconscious mind and have used it both to implant information in the brain and to draw it forth again when required.

Furthermore, occult teaching of whatever persuasion — Eastern or Western, Hermetic, Christian or Pantheistic — avers that there is only a limited number of basic energies or Universal Forces at large in the Cosmos. Most ancient faiths represented these Universal Forces to themselves in anthropomorphic guise because they recognized them to be not just immensely powerful, but also purposive and intelligent. They therefore personified these energies as beings like themselves, though often taller and more imposing, because they knew of no other species that possessed reasoning powers similar to their own. These personifications became the gods and goddesses of the various pantheons, while the monotheistic faiths — Judaism, Christianity and Islam — tended to label these energies 'Archangels'.

The Teutonic shaman began by postulating nine Universal Forces, just as the Egyptians built their religious system around an ennead (and this probably accounts for the resonance between Teutonic and Egyptian magic noted by Murry Hope and other researchers). These nine Universal Forces were identified with the Sun and the Moon, the five planets visible to the naked eye (as they had no telescopes the Teutons knew nothing about the planets beyond Saturn), and the North and South Nodes of the Moon. It is the modes of expression of these basic energies, combined with the functional alliances they form among themselves, that are embodied in the twenty-four Runes of the Elder Futhark.

In many ways, however, memorizing the meanings and attributions of each individual Rune is the easiest aspect of runic divination. The hardest part, as with any form of prognostication, is always interpretation. In order for any system of divination to work effectively it is necessary for it to contain enough symbols (or personifications of Universal Forces) to present its message unequivocally, but not so many as to make the feat of memory impossible. Sometimes the method of divination itself contains relatively few symbols, while at other times only a small number of symbols will be selected for interpretation. The less symbols employed by a divinatory system, either inherently or via the process of selection, the more the diviner is required to rely on his or her own intuition in order to interpret them.

The Mechanics of Intuition

Intuition is a natural ability and one which everyone possesses in some measure however small. Perhaps a greater understanding of the powers of intuition can be arrived at by examining some of mankind's other natural, though initially latent, abilities — abilities such as numeracy, literacy and manual dexterity, for all these share certain characteristics in common with the capacity to be intuitive.

First it should be noted that, although we all possess these talents, some people often display more aptitude in one particular area of ability than other people do. Secondly, none of these talents flourishes unless it is exercised, and if it is not exercised, it atrophies.

In my experience, the Runes are excellent developers and intensifiers of intuition. They have the power to free the psychic faculties from the restrictive bondage of temporal thought patterns. The fact that they are a form of Earth divination seems to make no difference to this power. On the contrary, the practical nature of the advice afforded by the Runes coupled with the intuitive insights sparked off by the symbols themselves makes a first-class combination.

Intuition may manifest itself in several ways, usually through one of the five senses acting at a more rarefied level, but often needing an aid — a trigger or starting handle. Generally, students developing intuition experience either clairvoyance, clairaudience or clairsentience — the psychic or astral equivalents of the physical senses of sight, hearing and touch. It is unusual for a divinatory system to stimulate the psychic senses of taste and smell, mainly because of the difficulties experienced in forming predictions through the medium of these sensations.

In the case of clairvoyance, or seeing with the astral eyes, the student perceives pictures or visions. During the period when the novice is still developing this ability, such pictures are often experienced as momentary flashes. Sometimes the 'vision' totally obliterates the material world, but most often it is as though the astral picture had been superimposed over the physical surroundings so that both types of sight are experienced simultaneously. The vision received may be static (like a photograph) or moving (like a cinema film). It may depict an actual future happening, or it may be purely symbolic. For example, to see a lamb may indicate that an event is due to occur at the lambing season, from March to April.

This description may sound strange to those of you who have not had this kind of experience yourselves. Like most aspects of the occult, it cannot be adequately described; it must be experienced. Imagine trying to tell someone from Alpha Centauri what strawberry ice cream tastes like and you will have a fair idea of what I mean!

Clairaudience, or hearing with the astral ears, works in much the same way. The student is aware of a word, a name, or even a whole sentence being spoken, and again, may have difficulty in distinguishing between physical sounds and astral sounds. Likewise, the type of voice, its clarity and volume, may differ from one occurrence to another; at times it may give direct information while at others it may speak symbolically.

The initial approaches of intuition, however, are most commonly made through the faculty of clairsentience, or the perception of astral sensations. Sometimes this develops into clairvoyance, sometimes into clairaudience and sometimes it simply remains itself. Clairsentience is the most common form of psychic perception, and perhaps the least well understood. Certainly it is the hardest to describe.

When working with clairsentience, a word or picture will often come to mind as the result of a strong presentiment being translated into some more appropriate term of reference. It is not so much that the student spontaneously 'sees' or 'hears', as that their feelings suggest certain auditory or visual images to them which they themselves convert into words or pictures. Once again this is a rather peculiar process to explain to anyone who has not shared the experience.

All I can say is that, whatever form your own personal intuitional faculty assumes in order to make contact with your conscious self, you will be able to recognize it from these descriptions *once you have experienced it*. It is a good idea, therefore, to return to this section when you reach the end of the first part of the book, and to re-read it to see if it throws any light on the intuitional experiences you will have been having.

Let me make it quite clear that none of these three types of intuition is superior to any other. All are equally useful once one has learnt to work with them. But it is only through the exercise of your own intuition that you will discover how it best works in your particular case, and it is only by testing and training your intuition that you will strengthen and develop it. And one of the best methods of training the intuition is through the practice of simple divinatory techniques such as those afforded by the runic system.

A Vocabulary of Runic Divination

Before we go on to examine the Runes individually, it is necessary that we familiarize ourselves with the vocabulary of divination and of runic divination in particular. There follows a set of definitions covering the most popularly used words and phrases in the field of divination together with an explanation of several terms peculiar to the runic system.

Reading

The term 'reading' covers the whole period given over to divination from the time you tip your Runes out of their bag until you have finished explaining to the enquirer exactly what they disclose.

More narrowly, whatever you tell your enquirer, whatever information you extract from the Runes on your own account constitutes a reading, while the person who gives the reading is called the 'reader'.

Runecast

The word 'runecast' is used to describe the pattern in which the Runes are laid out prior to divination. Runecast is often used in the same way as reading, expressions like 'to make a runecast' and 'to give a reading' being interchangeable. Sometimes referred to simply as a 'cast'.

Querent

Another term for the enquirer, the person who is consulting the Runes. In the initial stages of your studies you will be your own querent.

Positive/Negative

In these pages I have applied the terms Positive and Negative mainly to Runes. A positive Rune is one which promises happiness and fulfilment for the querent, either in the light of the question asked or in the context of the querent's present requirements. A negative Rune is one which withholds or prevents the attainment of success in some particular direction. These terms should not be confused with the concepts of good and evil. An enquirer may wish to marry someone who, though the querent does not realize it, would only bring them unhappiness and pain. Negative Runes might therefore turn up in the runecast to denote the querent's reaction to the alliance *not coming off*. Positive Runes, indicative of a lucky escape, would not appear, for it is the querent's *initial desire* that is taken into account by the runic forces and not the overall trend of the querent's life. This is due to the fact that, according to runic philosophy, the overall trend of evolution is always progressive.

Active/Passive
I have used the terms Active and Passive to refer to the action of the planetary forces when impacting singly on individual Runes. Where a planet in active mode has rulership over a Rune, it generally denotes the querent making his or her mark on the world, taking an active part in events, etc. Where a planet in passive mode has rulership over a Rune it usually shows things happening to the querent — which may be pleasant or unpleasant — but over which the enquirer has little or no control.

Upright/Reversed
A Rune may be either Upright (the right way up) or Reversed (upside down). With most Runes the upright and reversed positions are readily distinguishable and a Rune of this type generally has two distinct meanings. When it is the right way up a Rune should be considered Positive, and when it is in reverse it usually exhibits its more negative characteristics. For this reason, some runic diviners designate these positions Dignified and Ill-dignified.

Non-Reversible
With some Runes the reversed position would be indistinguishable from the upright one. These Runes are referred to as *non-reversible*. This is strictly inaccurate since all Runes are capable of being reversed. It is just that with these Runes it is impossible to tell the difference. But non-reversible is a handy expression, the use of which represents a great saving both in time and in words, and for this reason I have retained it.

Position
The word 'position' is only used to indicate 'position in a runecast'. The terms 'reversed' and 'upright' serve to describe the condition of a Rune, i.e. whether it is positive or negative in its results.

Result or Resultant Position
Many runecasts include a placement which indicates the result or outcome of the question under review. This placement may consist of either one Rune or a pair of Runes and is usually, though not always, the last Rune or pair of Runes to be laid out. Some Runes, particularly the non-reversible ones, have a slightly different or expanded meaning when they fall in the 'Result Position', while others are strengthened in their significance by being thus placed.

Prominent Position
In some runecasts certain sectors may be more important than others. For instance, the Result Position, if there is one, will always be of primary interest to your querent. On other occasions, where the querent prefers not to state their problem directly, the section which reveals what the enquirer has on their mind may assume a special relevance to you as the Reader. In some runecasts

the central symbol colours the whole of the rest of the reading.

What does or does not constitute a prominent position can vary from reading to reading, and as you gain experience you will find that *any* placement can attain the status of a prominent position simply by virtue of the fact that, as you turn over that particular Rune something 'clicks' in your subconscious which tells you: 'This is the one. This is the root of the problem.'

Chapter 3

THE ELDER FUTHARK

The Concept of Fate

In modern runic divination one piece is left blank. In so far as all the early Runes were glyphs or symbols, this 'Blank Rune' cannot truly be thought of as a Rune at all. On the other hand, since all Runes represent *secrets*, and the Blank Rune also conceals a mystery, it is possible to make a case for it to be permitted to bear that title.

The concept of the Blank Rune is a modern one and has come into being in order to represent an idea that was not fully understood by the ancient Teutonic shaman. It is a mistake to assume that the Initiates of former times knew more than we do about *all* aspects of occult science and that this superior knowledge has been lost to us through subsequent supression, willing or unwilling. Mankind is a still-evolving unit, at least so far as his mental faculties are concerned, and the man in the street is now able to look with equanimity on many of the concepts which would have seemed revolutionary to his ancestors. This statement is true in every other field of human endeavour, so there is no reason to suppose that occultism constitutes any sort of special case in this matter.

Early man tended to believe that all things rested in the hands of the gods (or Universal Forces) and that the individual had no control whatsoever over his or her own destiny. Today we view things rather differently. The materialist accepts the limitations imposed on him by such Universal Forces as gravity and heredity but determines to work within this framework to create for himself the kind of life to which he aspires. The occultist, too, believes much the same sort of thing, though he acknowledges the existence of underlying forces other than those at present catalogued by science. The occultist also believes in another force, a force which he is powerless to oppose and which, if he is so foolhardy as to attempt to do so, will lead him into a war of attrition that he must inevitably lose.

This force is usually called *Karma*, which name relates directly to the concept of reincarnation. Karma is a Sanskrit word meaning literally 'action', and it is borrowed by modern Western occultists from their Eastern cousins to denote the esoteric aspect of a well known exoteric law more usually applied to the science of physics: 'For every action in the Universe there must be an equal and opposite reaction.' Thus, according to the occult philosophy of Karma, every action a person makes eventually ricochets back on them. Each of us, therefore, bears the ultimate responsibility for his or her own fate. This our Teutonic ancestors well understood. What they did not understand was the extent to which they were able to control their own individual destinies. And what the modern mind does not yet comprehend is the exact extent to which our destinies, through the agency of Karma, control us.

I intend to deal with the Blank Rune first before moving on to examine the Alphabet Runes of the Elder Futhark proper. I have chosen this approach because the Blank Rune has a quite specific meaning when it appears in the runecast outlined at the end of this chapter, and it seems to me only logical to have all the information relevant to this Rune available in one place. But by taking the Blank Rune first, it has not been my intention to imply that this piece stands at the head of the Elder Futhark and corresponds to Zero, like the Fool in the Tarot pack. This is not the case at all. The Blank Rune stands apart from the Alphabet Runes and is allocated no number, neither the cypher Zero nor any of the numerals. Perhaps the best way of explaining the Blank Rune to a science-fiction generation is to say that it operates from another dimension to that in which the Elder Futhark has its sphere of activity. It represents the X in the equation of human endeavour, that which cannot adequately be allowed for or explained by our view of the world *in its present state.*

Alternatives	: —
Letter	: —
Name	: WYRD
Meaning	: Fate
Planetary Rulership	: The Part of Fortune

The Blank Rune is called WYRD (pronounced *weird*) which is the collective name given to the Three Norns, the Three Fates of Teutonic mythology. Their individual names are Urd, Verdandi and Skuld, and they represent the three aspects of ever-flowing Time: Past, Present and Future. They form a Trinity, forever dissolving one into another. The Wyrd rule over the Karma that each one of us has accrued during our past incarnations (or — for those who are not attracted to the doctrine of reincarnation — in our lives to date).

In divination, this Rune indicates those events which are fated or inevitable and which cannot be evaded. We must not, however, make the mistake of equating 'fated' with 'fatal'. After all, we must allow that there are two kinds of Karmic debt, the good and the bad (or, as I prefer to call them, the pleasant and the unpleasant), and we must not jump to the conclusion that the appearance of this Rune in a runecast heralds a Karmic punishment rather than a Karmic reward. Much depends on the accompanying Runes, and if it is the type of runecast in which the Runes are read by pairs, then the symbol associated with WYRD should be especially noted in this respect.

For instance, if WYRD falls with a Love-rune, such as GEOFU, it suggests that the querent is destined to make a happy alliance that is the reward for some unselfish or truly loving action in their Karmic past. Often this action has constituted a sublimation of the enquirer's own feelings so that the loved-one might be free to embrace their own version of happiness. What it would *not* mean is that the two protagonists are held together by a karmic link, that they were 'made for each other', or had 'been together in a former life'. These things do happen, but not so often as some people would like to imagine.

To the concept of *fated* and *fatal* we can add the concept of *fateful*, for when the Blank Rune falls in a prominent position in a runecast it indicates that, if a certain step should be taken, life will never be the same again for the querent. According to the type of question asked, this may refer to some action contemplated by the querent, or to an event foreshadowed by the runecast itself. But in either event, the Blank Rune is ambiguous since it could just as easily be presaging a disastrous occurrence as a pleasurable one. It is best to look to the following Runes, especially the Result Rune if there is one, to judge the desirability or otherwise of following out a particular course of action. And if the Blank Rune is itself in the Result position, be careful not to colour your interpretation with your own desires: remember the old proverb, 'Those whom the gods wish to destroy they first make mad.'

Because the Blank Rune signifies those things which are predestined or unavoidable, it can also represent anything which must be kept secret or remain undisclosed *for the querent's own good*. It is in this context that the Rune is used in the runecast given at the end of this chapter. Likewise, the Blank Rune signifies those incidents relating to the private lives of other people about which we have no right to be curious, and it is frequently prominent in a runecast where the querent is demanding access to information about someone else which is not really any of their concern.

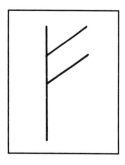

Alternatives	:	Þ Ⱶ
Letter	:	F
Name	:	FEOH
Meaning	:	Cattle
Planetary Rulerships	:	Venus and the Moon

In divination, the primary meaning of FEOH is wealth. As explained in Chapter 2, prior to the invention of money, a person's standing was measured by the size of their herds, so that cattle became irrevocably linked with the idea of substance or wealth in the Teutonic mind. In English we still retain the word *fee*, which the dictionary defines as 'a sum payable to officials': *fee* is the modern pronunciation of the Anglo Saxon *feoh*, the Viking *fe*, and must at one time have been paid in cattle.

Since cattle require a certain amount of looking after — moving from pasture to pasture, regular milking and the like — FEOH generally indicates earned income. Because the breeding of cattle produces more cattle (and not, for instance, elephants or falcons) FEOH also signifies an expected or anticipated monetary gain. If we translate the idea that 'cattle make cattle' into the economic principle that 'money makes money', it becomes obvious that, under certain conditions, FEOH can also indicate a successful financial investment.

In primitive agriculture oxen were used for ploughing. Thus FEOH indicates something gained through the expenditure of one's own energy: a conquest rather than a gift. It implies something fought or struggled for and is, therefore, a significator of opposition successfully overcome. This opposition may be of a personal kind and emanate from one particular opponent, or it may be of an impersonal kind and arise merely from adverse circumstances. Unless the rest of the Runes in the accompanying runecast are very negative indeed, the occurrence of FEOH upright suggests that the enquirer will eventually win out over opposing forces, especially when it falls in the Result position.

Because one of the planetary rulers of FEOH is Venus, the goddess of love, this Rune can also refer to an emotional gain or (bearing in mind that FEOH represents successful striving) a romantic conquest. Often it appears in a runecast when the querent is not quite sure if his or her feelings are returned or where there is a rival, or suspected rival, in love. In such a situation, FEOH signifies that a declaration of affection will be well received if only the querent can pluck up enough courage to make it. Or, as our Teutonic ancestors might have said, 'Faint heart never won fair lady.'

The other planet sharing joint rulership over this Rune is the Moon. She represents the Great Mother, the goddess of nature, once worshipped all over Western Europe. Many cultures represented the Moon as a cow, and cow's milk was sacred to her. The cow and her milk symbolized the Moon as the nourisher of mankind, an aspect of her maternal role. As the Great Mother, she was seen as a protective influence, for it is part of the mothering instinct to nourish and protect. She is, therefore, connected with the idea of preservation, both in the sense of 'to preserve from harm' and 'to preserve food for the winter-time', when nature's providence is temporarily curtailed. Along with the concept of preservation goes the allied concept of conservation.

Because of these associations, FEOH can indicate that the querent is passing through a period when it is necessary to conserve or consolidate his resources, whether material or physical. It signifies the successful development or completion of any projects already under way — but ventures still at the planning stage should be held in reserve. FEOH does not imply that these schemes should be abandoned; often they are basically sound and can be resurrected at a later time when circumstances are more auspicious.

Since a person who conserves is a conservative (with a small 'c'!), FEOH can be taken to signify a situation which calls for a conservative approach. This is particularly so when FEOH is paired with other Runes that represent caution. This Rune does not generally advise a new start of any kind but is more amenable to the progress of schemes or situations already embarked upon, no matter how recently. The only exception being in cases where the querent is contemplating a financial investment in some safe conservative area such as Blue Chip, National Savings Bonds, or the like.

When accompanied by negative Runes, FEOH advises against changing horses in mid-stream, though often predicting success in the matter in hand. FEOH regularly appears in a runecast to indicate that the querent has become discouraged, either in business or romance, and is contemplating a withdrawal from the present set-up with the intention of trying again elsewhere. Since FEOH contains within itself the concept of opposition, it is not unusual to find this Rune in association with others signifying obstacles and delay. As long as FEOH is upright, however, it indicates eventual success, and can be taken as an intimation to the querent not to throw in the towel while there is still a chance of victory.

Reversed

Since, when upright, FEOH means 'gain or conquest if the course already embarked upon is adhered to', in reverse it will mean 'loss or failure if the course already embarked upon is adhered to'.

FEOH reversed presages difficulties and frustrations in money matters. The opposition portended by the upright Rune is now too strong, at least for the present, and the querent is likely to be overwhelmed by it. In questions relating to love or marriage, FEOH reversed signifies emotional trouble and heartache. It often betokens disagreements and arguments which lead to a lack or breach of harmony. Sometimes this aggression can culminate in a separation and the break up of the relationship. With other, positive Runes in the majority, however, it may indicate that these disruptions are only temporary.

When the general tone of the reading is otherwise positive, or when FEOH is paired with a positive Rune, its main signification is delay: the time is not yet ripe for the querent's plans to come to fruition. In a negative reading, or in association with a negative Rune, however, it indicates that any plan already underway should be given up since it is not likely to prove successful no matter how much time, energy or money is invested in it.

We can, therefore, sum up the meanings of FEOH reversed by saying that it denotes a period in which one will experience great difficulty in consolidating or retaining one's financial or emotional status.

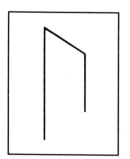

Alternatives	: ∏ ∏
Letter	: U
Name	: UR
Meaning	: An Aurochs
Planetary Rulership	: Mars (Passive)

The aurochs (*bos primigenius*) was a wild bison, now extinct, somewhat like the North American buffalo, and once common in Northern Europe. The youths of the Germanic tribes used to hunt the aurochs, and not until they had participated in a successful kill were they reckoned to have proved their manhood. Only then were they permitted to join the ranks of the warriors and go into battle with the other men of the tribe. The planet Mars, held by the ancient Germanic shaman to equate with the symbol UR, is also a significator of masculine energy, and bearing these two factors in mind, it is easy to understand the meanings allotted to UR in a runecast.

Because the young men proved themselves by killing the aurochs, it indicates a chance to prove oneself. Because their action elevated them from the ranks of children under the authority of their parents to the station of free men, UR also represents any sudden or dramatic change in one's circumstances — especially one which places the querent in a new or untried situation, or which throws him upon his own resources. Although the original symbolism applied exclusively to a male test of strength, all the meanings in this paragraph are just as appropriate to a female querent as to a male one.

UR often appears in a runecast to denote a promotion or an added responsibility in some direction. Since the aurochs could not be killed without strength and fighting skill, this Rune also indicates that the querent possesses both the energy and the innate ability required to handle the change or shoulder the forthcoming responsibility.

Sometimes, the querent sees the change signalled by this Rune as a somewhat daunting one. This is only natural: like the Germanic adolescents setting out into the unfamiliar territory of adulthood, they are leaving the security of the known for the exciting but frightening world of unknown possibilities. Often there is a need for sacrifice — not an unwilling or injurious sacrifice, but an exchange of the lesser good for the greater good. It is indicative of something in the querent's life that once was good, but which has had its day and is now destined to be replaced by new and beneficent conditions. The keynote of this Rune is natural change. Therefore, as adolescence replaces childhood to be itself replaced by maturity, the changes heralded by this Rune should not — indeed, cannot — be evaded.

Being a martian Rune, UR indicates many of the positive virtues of Mars which, in previous centuries, have been seen as the prerogative of the male: energy, will-power, determination, true grit. (In the book and film of that name, it should be noted, it is the *girl* who exhibits the quality of 'true grit', thus proving that either sex can display a fighting temperament when conditions warrant it.)

Energy displays itself not only as combative spirit but also as vitality and rude health. It is an excellent sign for this Rune to appear upright where any question relating to health has been posed, since it signifies great stamina and strong natural powers of resistance.

Because Mars is a planet having rulership over the male sex, UR often represents the male partner in a love affair or marriage — and this rule applies irrespective of whether the querent is male or female. In such cases, UR indicates the man's sex urge, and suggests that passion is running high on the male side.

In business and financial questions, this Rune indicates that an improvement in the querent's present situation is to be expected, but only through the application of will-power and effort. It is not a Rune which suggests that all your troubles will be taken from your shoulders by an indulgent benefactor: it is more a Rune of standing on one's own feet.

Reversed

Usually the message of UR reversed is: do not let an opportunity to show what you can do slip through your fingers.

In a mainly negative runecast, however, it can sometimes mean: this is an opportunity you *should* allow to pass you by.

If UR is reversed but the Rune associated with it promises change (RAD or EOH, for instance), it suggests there will be insufficient drive or ability (or both) to bring matters to a successful conclusion. Counsel the querent against making such a change, and look to the other Runes in the cast to see whether they imply a cancellation of present plans or merely a postponement.

UR reversed can also indicate an unfortunate turn of events. Sometimes, as with the upright interpretation, it may presage a sweeping change, but one that, in this case, is not to the querent's liking. Despite appearances to the contrary, things may eventually turn out for the best if UR falls with positive Runes.

The reversal of this Rune can signify weak will-power, and sometimes shows the possibility of the querent falling under the influence of a stronger personality. It is particularly to be feared in this context when paired with a partnership Rune such as GEOFU or WYNN reversed, or when falling in the Seventh House of an Astrological runecast.

It also stands for low vitality — which may be responsible for an illness or be a contributory factor towards an illness. In addition to which, for a male querent, it may indicate medical or psychological problems of a sexual nature.

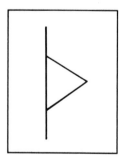

Alternatives	: Þ ᛒ ᚦ
Letter	: Th
Name	: THORN
Meaning	: A Thorn
Planetary Rulerships	: Jupiter (Active)

Plants grow thorns to protect themselves, and in astrology, Jupiter is a protective planet. The Teutonic equivalent to Jupiter was Thor, who was the Great Protector of Northern mythology. The later Teutons often used to wear a small representation of the Hammer of Thor around their necks just as the Christians wore a Cross, and for much the same reasons. It would seem then, that THORN is a lucky Rune, signifying help and protection; but this is not always the case, though THORN can have such a meaning if it falls in association with another protective Rune such as YR or EOLH (both of which are also ruled by Jupiter).

Sometimes, in an otherwise fortunate runecast, THORN will herald a totally unexpected stroke of good luck. Occasionally this will take the form of assistance from a parent, friend, or superior, but more often than not it is a genuine 'lucky break' resulting from one of those strange concatenations of circumstance that are usually described as 'being in the right place at the right time'.

To the plant that sports it, the thorn is a defence; but to the unwary nature-lover it is a warning. And it is in this guise that THORN generally appears in a runecast. It tends to come up when the querent has had a run of good luck and is acting as if it will never end. The querent either wants to continue expanding his sphere of influence, or is indulging in uncontrolled extravagance. The warning implicit in THORN then is: take stock of your situation and consolidate your position before attempting to make further progress.

The appearance of THORN in a runecast often suggests that the querent is being wrong-headed in some direction, and the associated Runes will indicate whether that direction is to do with business, emotions, or finance. In such a case, the advice afforded by this Rune is that one should do nothing new or innovative, make no unnecessary changes, but attempt to keep the situation as it is until the end of the period covered by the reading (or, in the Gate of Heaven runecast, until the Runes indicate that it would be safe to proceed). This is particularly true when THORN is associated with, or surrounded by, HAGALL, NIED or IS.

In circumstances where the querent is being pressurized to make a decision or to take some sort of action, it is obvious that the injunction 'do nothing' cannot apply. When this is so, the presence of THORN suggests that one should do nothing *off one's own bat*. Jupiter rules lawyers, solicitors, bankers, doctors and priests — all the so-called 'professions' — so, where necessary, the querent should seek professional advice, especially if THORN falls in association with ANSUR, JARA or MANN.

In short, we can say that when THORN projects the negative side of its nature in a runecast, it means that the querent is opposed by those who are politically, financially, or morally stronger than he is himself. This ascendancy may or may not last according to whether the other Runes in the reading are helpful or unhelpful.

Reversed
The meaning of THORN reversed is much the same as when it is upright. The main difference is that you may have more difficulty in persuading the querent to take your advice. THORN reversed usually indicates that the querent is set on some particular course of action and is unwilling to listen to the advice of others. Often, this leads to quarrels with those people who are attempting to advise or direct the querent. Also, when THORN is reversed, the consequences of stubbornly following one's own path are likely to be even more disastrous than when the Rune is the right way up. The enquirer must learn that man proposes but God disposes!

Sometimes, THORN reversed indicates that the querent is in a senior or authoritative position and views the development of an underling as a threat. This interpretation applies not only in a business context, but to parent and child, guardian and ward, teacher and pupil. Look for the presence of KEN reversed as denoting that one party is about to be outgrown or surpassed by the other.

On the other hand, the querent may fear that a protégé will fail in some test, and that this failure will reflect badly upon the enquirer as manager, trainer, teacher or instructor.

In any event, we can say that THORN reversed presages the onset of a period when one's luck is out, and caution and circumspection are the order of the day.

Alternatives	:	
Letter	: A	
Name	: ANSUR	
Meaning	: A Mouth	
Planetary Rulership	: Mercury (Passive)	

ANSUR means a 'mouth' and, by association, it implies the spoken word. This in turn connects with Mercury's position in all pantheons as the god of eloquence and intelligence. We have already noted that the Teutonic shaman passed on their knowledge by word of mouth. Thus, the spoken word may also be seen as the repository of wisdom and knowledge, the medium by which education and knowledge are imparted and retained: even as late as Edwardian times the English educational system leaned heavily on the process of learning by rote.

Mercury, in Aryan astrology, is always called 'a boy', signifying one who has yet to prove his manhood; one who is not yet out of tutelage. When a planet is allocated rulership of a Rune in its passive mode, it usually depicts the querent receiving the qualities of that planet from another source. For this reason, ANSUR generally indicates the querent's acquisition of wisdom and knowledge, the seeking and taking of advice, rather than the dispensing of such qualities.

In the sphere of education, ANSUR can also mean a spoken test, as in the *viva voce*. By extension, this may be taken to signify any verbal examination such as an interview — or, in fact, any kind of test, oral, written or practical. It may even refer to a testing experience thrown up by life itself. Most new experiences comprise a test of some sort, and ANSUR upright indicates that the querent will come through the test, or pass the examination, with flying colours.

All the attributions of a passive Mercury suggest apprenticeship. This may be construed in a formal sense as apprenticeship to a trade, or more loosely as having reference to an aspect of life of which the querent has no previous experience. In the old system of apprenticeship, the novice learned by observing the master and receiving the master's instructions. All of which leads us back to the idea of tutelage.

To be under tutelage suggests that the enquirer will receive instruction or advice or some more tangible form of assistance from a parent or parental figure. This latter may, for example, be a teacher, whom the law states as being in *loco parentis* (standing in place of a parent); or it may indicate someone older and thus (presumably) wiser, or someone in a superior position: an employer (often the querent's immediate boss, since this Rune rarely denotes an impersonal, faceless entity), or anyone having superior knowledge. This is usually someone who has undergone some sort of training themselves — like a doctor, a lawyer, an accountant, a surveyor, an electrician, a plumber, etc.

ANSUR is indicative of unbiased or honest advice. Because it is ruled by Mercury passive, it denotes the need for deliberation prior to action, and often signals the need to take advice before committing oneself further. For instance: in an Astrological runecast, ANSUR in the Sixth, Eighth or Twelfth House may intimate that a timely check up by the doctor could halt an infection in its early stages. In the Twelfth House it can also point to the need for counselling — the querent has often got himself into a needless muddle and needs to talk matters out with a trained advisor.

Mercury has rulership over movement and journeys, though this is more properly the domain of Mercury active. Only rarely will this Rune indicate a journey by the querent, unless it shows a journey that is made in order to gain news of a relative, or to seek instruction. Since it acts passively, this Rune is more likely to mean a visit *from* a parent or relative, and the Rune paired with ANSUR will often show the kind of person involved, though here much depends on the querent's circumstances. For instance, BEORC signifies a relative, but this may be the querent's mother, if she is still alive, or one of the querent's children, assuming he has any. If the associated Rune is JARA, the person indicated is likely to be a lawyer or solicitor; and if OTHEL, an aged relative.

Reversed

When reversed ANSUR represents biased advice. Parents or relatives selfishly want what is best for themselves and not what is best for the enquirer; workmen give false or unreliable quotes or attempt to overcharge; professional advice cannot be relied upon to be impartial. In this respect, ANSUR reversed often signifies that the advisor in question has become too closely involved in the problem and can no longer maintain an impersonal stance.

ANSUR reversed is also indicative of trickery, lies and misinformation generally. The querent should believe nothing he hears (or reads, come to that) and should be urged to take a second opinion in all matters of importance.

In reverse, this Rune can suggest that parents or superiors are trying to interfere adversely with the querent's plans. Sometimes, though, it indicates that older people may present difficulties through the circumstances of their lives rather than through active opposition; that they may become a burden or a worry through no fault of their own — due to illness, for example.

It can also mean a wasted journey; the misuse of knowledge and wisdom by the querent; or troubles with studies. These troubles may occur in an academic context, or the reversal of ANSUR may simply imply a refusal to learn life's lessons. Note carefully where the Blank Rune falls in relation to ANSUR before making a judgement on this point.

With other negative Runes, ANSUR reversed often indicates that the querent is an 'eternal student', one who wants to go on gathering more and more knowledge without the slightest intention of ever passing it on either by practical application or by precept. It is the 'Peter Pan' attitude of one who is unwilling to pass on into maturity and (like Mercury, the boy) is unable to act as a father to either deeds or ideas.

Divination Practice
Asking the Norns

This simple runecast is an excellent way to answer all 'Yes or No' questions. There are not many enquiries that do not fall into this category since most people want to know such things as: 'Should I change my job?', 'Should I marry my present lover?', and 'Will the sale of my house go through without mishap?'.

Asking the Norns will enable you to answer these questions, and others like them, clearly and accurately. As you become more experienced — and add more Runes to the five you will be starting with — you will find that you are able to dispense with the 'Yes or No' format and can Ask the Norns for their advice on any predicament in which you or your Querents happen to find yourselves.

What it will not do, however, is answer multiple questions such as 'Will I marry John and be happy?'. This is not one question, but two, and they should be dealt with separately.

Method

Following the instructions on page 29, lay out your diviner's cloth and place the Runes face downwards on it. Swirl the Runes, select three, and lay them in front of you as shown in Figure 5.

Turn over all three Runes and note how many are upright and how many reversed. This will give you the general tenor of the reading. Upright Runes have a positive or helpful influence, and reversed Runes have a negative, or inhibiting, influence. When you start working with non-reversible Runes, you will need to remember which are positive and which are negative, though non-reversible Runes are the ones most easily influenced by the Runes with which they find themselves associated.

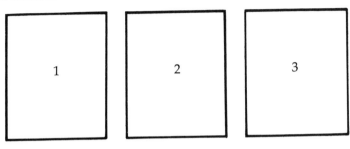

Figure 5: Asking the Norns

When all three Runes are positive, the answer is an unqualified 'Yes'. When they are all negative, the answer is 'No'; but the Runes selected will usually indicate why you have received this answer, and will often advise you what to do to improve your chances of success.

If you or your Querent have chosen a mixture of positive and negative Runes, you will need to do a little more work to get an intelligible reply. Much depends on how relevant the positive Rune or Runes are to the type of question asked. For example, it is not much good having ANSUR upright in your runecast if you have asked 'Will I win this year's Irish Sweepstake?', since winning the Irish Sweepstake is not dependent on brain-power. What the Runes are probably telling you is: 'If you care to think about it, the answer will be obvious.'

Where there are two positive Runes and one negative one in the runecast, the implication is that although the answer to the question is 'Yes', there will be some aspect of the situation that does not come up to your, or your Querent's, expectations. Imagine that a male Querent asks: 'Will I be able to sell my car easily?' He chooses two positive Runes, plus FEOH reversed. While the answer is affirmative, the enquirer will be required to drop his price, since FEOH signifies money.

When two Runes are negative, and one is positive, the answer is 'No', but the Querent may not come out of the situation as badly as they might — though this may prove cold comfort at the time of the reading.

Two negative Runes with a non-reversible Rune will probably sour the indications of the latter, and should be taken to express a definite 'No', as if there were three negatives involved.

The appearance of WYRD in this runecast has a special significance. It implies either that the question is not yet ready to be judged, too many variables still needing to be settled before a reliable reply can be given; or that the Norns feel that the Querent would be better off not knowing the answer to

that particular question. If you or your Querent should draw WYRD as one of
the three Runes when Asking the Norns, you are advised to wait at least three
hours (and preferably until the following day) before asking again. If the Blank
Rune still comes up, you may wait a further three hours, or another day, and
ask again. If WYRD appears on the third occasion, you must be content to wait
for events to unravel themselves without the benefit of foresight. Go no
further with your enquiries — or you may discover something not to your
liking.

WYRD frequently occurs in runecasts where the wrong type of question has
been asked. Questions like: 'Will I be happy if I change my job?' mean
different things to different people. To some, 'happiness' will mean a better
chance of promotion; to others, working with congenial colleagues; and to yet
others, an opportunity for romance. In my experience, a judicious alteration of
the *form* in which the question is put will result in an unequivocal answer at the
second attempt.

Chapter 4

RUNIC PROPORTIONS

Runes that were intended for use in divination or magic were always drawn to specific proportions. These proportions were: four units high by one and a half units wide or, with the broader Runes, three ($1\frac{1}{2}$ × 2) units wide. All the illustrations in Part One are drawn to this scale and most of the diagrams in Part Two also follow this pattern, though it is sometimes permissible to ignore this rule when designing Bindrunes. Figure 6 shows a series of examples of how individual Runes are drawn using this 4 × $1\frac{1}{2}$ framework.

Runes used for secular inscriptions do not always follow these laws of proportion and it is certain that the majority of the Teutonic people knew next to nothing about the more abstruse side of runic geometry. Like most of the geometry of the ancient world, this was symbolic in content, hardly concerning itself with such mundane preoccupations as the calculation of distance and area.

The Rune EOH is the only character to depart from the basic pattern of four rectangles one unit high by one and a half units wide. The downward strokes of this Rune are made to form a more obtuse angle with the two uprights than is usual. This means that their junction point is only half a unit from the topmost point of the Rune, whereas all the other symbols work only in full units vertically.

Herein lies a numerical clue to the meanings of the dimensions allotted to the runic letters, for half units are not a valid measure in Sacred Geometry. We must, therefore, divide all the units of runic proportion by two in order to get at the true scale employed by the Teutonic shaman. This division produces a rectangle 8 units by 3 units. Eight is the number of Destiny; and the number Three, when found rubbing shoulders with the number Eight, is generally indicative of the influence of the three Norns who, as we have seen, are the old Teutonic goddesses of Fate.

Some students may wish to make their own set of Runes, in which case they should attempt to adhere as closely as possible to the model of Figure 6 and the other illustrations of the Runes in Part One of this book. In later sections dealing with the magical uses of the Runes, it is even more important that one should stay strictly within the confines of runic proportions, for the Runes are carefully designed psychological triggers and inelegant or inharmonious proportions can unleash some unpleasant phenomena, such as those darker aspects of the libido which the Nordic peoples depicted to themselves in the forms of the avaricious dragon Fafnir and the destructive wolf Fenrir.

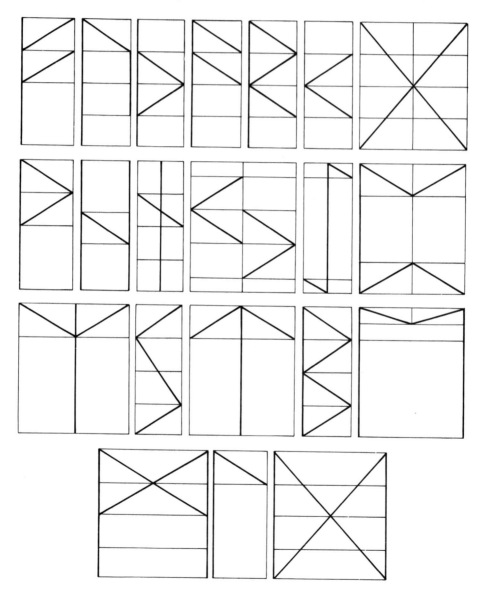

Figure 6: Runic Proportions — a selection

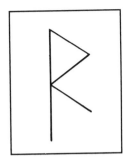

Alternatives	: ᛁ²
Letter	: R
Name	: RAD
Meaning	: A Cartwheel
Planetary Rulerships	: Mercury and the North Node

Like ANSUR, this Rune is under the dominion of Mercury. But here the Mercurial influence is mixed with that of the North Node which rules all things that are foreign or alien, unusual or unexpected, so that by this combination, another aspect of Mercury's character is emphasized.

Both Mercury and his Norse equivalent, Odin, are associated with travel. Mercury was called the 'Messenger of the Gods' and was the protector of all messengers, while Odin (who in myth regularly disguises himself as a wayfarer) was the god of travellers to the Germanic peoples. This accords with the meaning of RAD, a cartwheel, which also implies movement from one place to another. Thus RAD is a Rune of travel, usually signifying a journey for pleasure. This may be a visit to friends, a holiday, or any journey with some celebratory event at the end of it. Sometimes, this Rune signifies a safe and pleasant journey, one with no delays, accidents or frustrations; and instead of friends and a celebration on arrival, it can indicate a convivial travelling companion, or companions.

In early times, the only way a message could be delivered was by hand, or by word of mouth if the sender of the message was unable to write. Therefore, as well as its active meaning 'to go on a journey', RAD has the passive meaning 'to receive a message'. Nowadays we have many ways in which news may arrive, and RAD can denote any of these: telephone, telegram, letter — but do not overlook the spoken word because this is one of Mercury's primary correspondences as we can tell from his rulership of ANSUR, a mouth. Due to the influence of the North Node, which occludes or masks, the message may not be given face to face, though still delivered by word of mouth. The modern method of communication which best answers this description is the telephone; so at the present time RAD most often indicates a telephone message when signifying receipt of news. Also, due to the shared rulership of the North Node, the message may be unexpected or sudden. Either the news itself is unexpected, or it comes at an unexpected time.

Because of Mercury's close connection with the spoken word, RAD may also indicate that the period covered by the reading is a good one in which to enter into discussions or negotiations. In this context, the North Node represents the other person's point of view, while Mercury signifies that a flexible and reasonable attitude will prevail. Therefore, in all questions relating to a difference of opinion, RAD's appearance in a runecast suggests that, though there may have to be concessions on both sides, a satisfactory and mutually beneficial solution can be agreed.

Since RAD indicates movement, we may extend this idea to cover any form of action. This Rune may, therefore, signify that any action contemplated by the querent should be executed *now* (or in the month signified by the position held by RAD in the Gate of Heaven runecast), for this Rune is a fortunate omen, indicating that the querent can confidently proceed with his schemes. Because Mercury is a planet connected with mental effort, RAD can also signify that the querent is passing through a period conducive to all forms of logical thought: tactics, strategy, and the formulation and revision of plans in general.

Besides the messengers or seekers of news, other travellers in primitive times included traders and merchants, and due to this association with commerce, RAD often indicates that now is a good time either for buying or selling, as far as the querent is concerned. It may also presage a business trip — especially when paired with other business or money Runes.

Since the North Node has a tendency to cloud the issue, RAD will sometimes indicate an ambivalent or ambiguous situation. Both Mercury and Odin are associated with trickery and deception. Mercury was the patron of thieves and liars, and Odin had a reputation for being an expert riddler. He was also known as a shape-shifter — for appearing to be what he was not. So with adverse Runes, RAD can be a warning that the querent should place no faith in the spoken word of others, and that even the written word may play him false. He should read through all documents or contracts, paying particular attention to the proverbial 'small print'; and he should satisfy himself that the words mean what he takes them to mean. Other Runes in the cast will probably reveal wherein the danger lies; for instance: if PEORTH reversed is paired with RAD, it indicates a broken promise; if EOLH reversed is the paired Rune, the querent is in danger of being taken for a ride.

RAD can also indicate that the querent is in two minds about a certain course of action. Often the enquirer is in the position of Buridan's ass, where both propositions look equally inviting and the querent cannot decide which one to accept. This may relate to a choice between two lovers, or two jobs or career opportunities, either of which the querent feels could turn out well.

As we saw when examining ANSUR, Mercury has rulership over education, and RAD may occasionally refer to formal learning, education, study, exams, or teaching. But this is very much an ancillary meaning which usually only applies where RAD is actually paired with ANSUR, when it reinforces the symbolism of the latter Rune. Sometimes even then, the appearance of RAD will refer to its primary meaning of travel, implying that it will be necessary for the prospective student to leave home in order to attend university, college, polytechnic, or whatever.

Reversed
All the areas designated by RAD upright take on an unfortunate significance when the Rune is reversed.

It can indicate that the need to make a journey arises at an inconvenient time, or for an inconvenient reason. Often, it signifies a sudden journey to visit a sick friend or relative. Alternatively, RAD reversed can mean that friends or relatives may themselves decide to make a visit at an inopportune time.

For the traveller, it can indicate difficulties in transit: delays, breakdowns, crashes, missed connections, losing one's way, losing or mislaying one's luggage — in short, any of the problems attendant upon travelling today.

No matter what the area inquired about may be, RAD reversed shows the querent's schemes being upset. No matter how well-laid plans may be, some unforseen contingency will cause them to go awry.

Intransigence causes negotiations to break down. Or arguments occur because each party is intent on putting their own point of view without any consideration for the other people involved.

The normally quick-witted Mercury is made sluggish and ineffective by RAD's reversal. In consequence, the querent is likely to be the loser in commercial transactions, sometimes through deliberate trickery, sometimes through not displaying an on-the-ball, businesslike attitude.

Alternatives	: Ϝ ᚲ ᚴ ᚷ ᚺ
Letter	: K
Name	: KEN
Meaning	: A Torch
Planetary Rulerships	: Mars and the Sun

Mars is a planet that has much to do with springtime. The Romans, for instance, held their great festival to Mars at the Vernal Equinox, often called 'the first day of spring'. This is the period in the Sun's yearly cycle when new life flows over the land and, by analogy, KEN can equally be said to represent energy, strength, power and positivity.

Both Mars and the Sun are connected with fire, and in the days when the letters of the Futhark got their names, a torch would have been a simple firebrand — a branch of wood lit at one end. Fire gives off heat, and this can be associated with the heat given off by the body. By temperature we can ascertain the vitality and natural stamina of a person. KEN, therefore, is a significator of good health and strong powers of recuperation. Because KEN represents positivity on any level, it suggests that a positive attitude will aid recovery.

As in health questions this Rune indicates recovery, so by extension it can be taken to mean recovery from an adverse condition. For this reason, it is one of the most helpful symbols to appear in a runecast whenever the querent is experiencing difficulties of any sort.

Most ancient cultures used to think that the year began at the Vernal Equinox, and the start of the fiscal or tax year at the beginning of April is a remnant of this belief. It is also said — even amidst the artificial conditions of today's society — that 'in the spring, a young man's fancy lightly turns to thoughts of love'. The association of these two ideas — 'new' and 'love' — means that KEN's appearance in a runecast often heralds a new emotional relationship.

Because KEN stands for all forms of positivity, this Rune will usually indicate the positive or active partner in a relationship. In a sexual context, therefore, KEN will signify the man, no matter what sex the querent may be. And because fire gives out heat, it will often represent the male partner giving, or at least offering, something to the female partner. This may be a small gift or an expensive present; an offer of help or a proposal of marriage — or a very different type of proposition entirely.

But KEN can represent the active partner in any polarized relationship. In relationships other than sexually oriented ones, the active partner is the one in the superior position; the person in charge of, or otherwise having control over, the receptive partner. This may be parent to child, teacher to pupil, employer to employee, but it retains the same meaning as it does for a love relationship: a gift or offer from the person represented by the active pole to the person who is representing the passive pole.

If the querent is the passive person in the relationship, the Runes associated with KEN will indicate whether the gift or offer should be accepted, and what motives are likely to lie behind it.

Where the querent is the active partner in the relationship, the associated Runes will show whether or not the proposal will be accepted.

Animals are afraid of fire, and primitive man soon discovered that he could protect himself at night by building a fire. Being a fire-rune, KEN is also seen as a protective influence. It is a lucky sign whenever it appears upright, indicating a period when the querent is protected from the difficulties and unpleasantnesses of life; or this protection may simply be that (as with UR upright) the querent will not be tried beyond his capacity or strength.

However, besides symbolizing terrestrial fire, KEN also represents the concept of Primal Fire. In Teutonic mythology, the Cosmos — both in its manifest and unmanifest aspects — was created when the active element, Fire, began to work upon the passive element, Ice. Thus KEN is a strongly creative Rune. And because the activity of Primal Fire created both manifest and unmanifest existence, the creativity betokened by KEN may be of either the body or the mind. The 'present' given by the man to the woman could be a child — and KEN upright with any of the Runes signifying physical fertility (BEORC, ING, HAGALL) will often presage a physical birth — while with Runes that imply linguistic or artistic ability (ANSUR, RAD, WYNN, EOLH), KEN indicates creative work inspired by physical love, as when Dante was inspired by Beatrice.

Reversed

KEN is no exception to the rule that when a Rune capable of reversal falls upside down in a runecast it signifies a reversal of its upright meanings.

Rather than 'new' or 'beginning', it suggests 'end' or 'termination'.

Rather than a gift or offer, it suggests loss, or an offer withdrawn. It may indicate loss of love, loss of friendship, loss of employment, loss of position, or loss of power. Always it implies loss of something by which the querent sets great store.

When KEN is associated with positive Runes, the loss may be only transitory: if loss of love, there will be a reconciliation; if loss of employment, another job will soon be found; if loss of a treasured possession, that too will be recovered.

With delay-runes such as IS, OTHEL reversed, or NIED either way up, KEN reversed sometimes indicates that the loss or misplacement of some item causes delay or acts as a stumbling block to progress with much attendant anxiety.

When this Rune appears in any runecast concerned with relationships (and this is not restricted to sexually orientated relationships alone) it often denotes two people who have grown apart from one another, or it may show that one partner — frequently the one who was originally considered passive or receptive — has outgrown the other. It may signify that the child has grown up and no longer requires parental control, or that the pupil has equalled or surpassed the teacher and has nothing further to learn from that source.

This situation is particularly painful in love and friendship because, unlike the other types of relationship described, there is no logical way of explaining what has gone wrong. Everyone supposes that the child and the pupil will one day pass beyond the governance of parent or teacher, but society expects that the husband and the wife will grow closer as time passes. Friends, too, grow apart for no other reason than that they are each developing along different lines, expanding into different areas of life.

In questions relating to love, marriage partners or close friendships, the pairing of KEN reversed with NIED (especially where the latter Rune is also reversed) indicates that the querent is clinging to a failing relationship, unable to accept that it has undergone a subtle but radical change. It should be pointed out to the enquirer that any attempt to hold onto the relationship will only bring heartache and unhappiness to both parties.

Alternatives	: ⅃ᴴ
Letter	: G
Name	: GEOFU
Meaning	: A Gift
Planetary Rulerships	: Venus (Active)

It is well known that Venus is the planet of love, but she also has rulership over all amicable partnerships. This is reflected in the symbol for GEOFU, in which two lines combine and seem to offer mutual support. In a runecast, therefore, GEOFU signifies a union or partnership of some kind, and this may take the form of a fortunate business partnership or a successful love union.

Since GEOFU means 'a gift', this Rune is often a significator of generosity being shown towards the querent. This may range from generosity of spirit to a gift of money; from a small token of appreciation to an expensive present.

It is more usual, however, for GEOFU to betoken an important development in an emotional relationship, since Venus's primary attribution is love. It is interesting to note in this respect that GEOFU is the only Rune whose symbol has filtered down to the present day — as the cross we put at the end of letters to our loved ones to signify a kiss.

Often the two aspects of love and generosity are combined, as when the Rune stands for a wedding or engagement, because on these occasions the couple are traditionally presented with gifts.

On a simpler level, GEOFU indicates unity of action and intention, the result of which is that the querent feels at one with the world, experiencing a deep sense of peace and contentment and, where there have been preceding difficulties, relief.

As GEOFU looks the same either way up, there is no reversed meaning, and you will have to use your intuition if you are to assess its message in a runecast accurately. Generally, it is a positive indication, and when falling in a position where it signifies a result, GEOFU is always a good sign.

One word of warning, however: this Rune has a habit of appearing in a runecast merely to denote what the reading is about. Thus, a woman whose marriage is breaking down might draw GEOFU, FEOH reversed, and RAD reversed when Asking the Norns. GEOFU tells us that she is concerned about her relationship with her husband, but it is the other two Runes that show how their relationship is likely to fare — FEOH reversed showing difficulty in maintaining the status quo and a possible deterioration due to a rival, and RAD reversed indicating plans upset, duplicity from others and an unpleasant choice or decision ahead. Here GEOFU is neither positive nor negative in its signification. It shows what particular area of life is on the querent's mind and nothing more. So you must take care not to be led astray by the presence of

GEOFU in a runecast. You should examine the accompanying Runes and listen to your intuition.

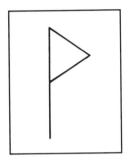

Alternatives   : ⸮
Letter   : W
Name   : WYNN
Meaning   : Joy
Planetary Rulerships : Venus and Saturn

Those students who know something of astrology may be a little perturbed to see that Saturn appears as one of the rulers of WYNN. Saturn, however, is a very deep planet with many facets to his character. He was pictured as a lame god, because he moved most slowly of all the planets known to the ancients, and is thus equivalent to Vulcan, the husband of Venus in Roman mythology, or Hephaistos, who holds the same position in the Greek Pantheon. Vulcan and Hephaistos were both lame gods. The marriage of Vulcan to Venus, Hephaistos to Aphrodite, explains why medieval writers on astrology referred to Saturn and Venus as 'secret friends', the true link having been forgotten. And aspects between Saturn and Venus are never as disastrous as Saturn's interactions with the other planets.

Because of the amity between Venus and Saturn, WYNN will always represent joy and happiness coming to the querent, and is an excellent omen to fall in a runecast — especially in the Result Position, where it presages an outcome that is both satisfactory and fortunate.

Since Vulcan is a smith, a workman (the Norse or Anglo-Saxon equivalent being Volund or Weyland, who was also a smith), this Rune can also represent joy in one's work, particularly where the work is creative and/or requires physical application. Creativity in this context refers mainly to work done with the hands rather than work requiring mental effort or dexterity — although the association of WYNN with ANSUR can bend the meaning in that direction. The appearance of WYNN in a runecast may sometimes indicate that the enquirer or the person enquired about is an artist, artisan, or craftsman.

Saturn's practicality and stolidity have a stabilizing effect on the flightiness of Venus, so that in combination with other Runes signifying romance, WYNN can indicate emotional happiness, and deep and lasting affection.

Because its meaning is joy, when WYNN falls with news-runes, it indicates the receipt of good news. Because, as far as the Teutonic astrologers were concerned, Saturn was the furthest planet from the Sun, this Rune often indicates that the news comes from a distance — possibly from abroad — while with a travel-rune, WYNN denotes that journeys abroad will be successful.

Often this Rune will represent the object of the enquirer's affections. Usually when it bears this connotation, it shows the loved one participating in some activity which leads to a joyous result. Depending on the associated Rune, this activity may involve travel or business — sometimes both.

In other instructions on runic divination, you may find this aspect of WYNN's meaning limited only to men. Usually, the delineation goes something like: a fair man who has recently returned from abroad, or who is required to travel in his job. This relates to a time when men travelled while women sat at home, and is no longer valid in those cultures where women have equal career opportunities with men. Likewise, the idea that WYNN describes a fair-haired person dates from early times when most Teutons were fair, and it can no longer be relied upon as an accurate indication of the colouring of either the querent or the person enquired about.

Reversed

When reversed, WYNN betokens misery and unhappiness. If the reading refers to travel, there will be unpleasantness on the journey, or the trip will not culminate successfully. If the reading refers to work, the querent will not be happy in his present employment, or will become dissatisfied with his own performance at work. If the reading refers to love, then the querent should expect a disappointment the magnitude of which (i.e. whether it will be a minor incident or a final break in the relationship) has to be judged from the associated Runes or from the Rune with which WYNN is paired.

When referring to a love affair or prospective business deal, WYNN reversed often indicates that a third party will cause trouble by using delaying tactics or encouraging friction between the two people concerned. It is a warning of double-dealing and clandestine arrangements engineered by opponents.

Whether the question relates to travel, business or romance, WYNN reversed signifies the need for caution, and wherever possible the querent should put off making any important decisions. Depending on the situation in which the querent is placed, this delay should be of days, weeks or months; and since the number associated with WYNN is six, then you should advise a delay of either six days, six weeks, or six months.

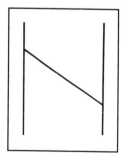

Alternatives	: ᛁᛁᛁᛁ ᛁᛁᛁ ✳
Letter	: H
Name	: HAGALL
Meaning	: Hail
Planetary Rulerships	: Saturn (Passive)

Astrologers say that Saturn is a planet of limitation, but they also call him 'the

Great Teacher'. The Teutonic shaman believed much the same thing, and combined these two attributions in the meaning they allotted to HAGALL. This meaning can be summed up as follows: understand that living in a material universe imposes certain natural limitations upon you; learn to live within these limitations and you will be happy. Since HAGALL is one of those Runes which look the same upright or reversed, we can say that this injunction is immutable, that the querent who adheres to it will be happy and successful, while the querent who ignores it will meet with distress and failure.

The mnemonic chosen by the Teutonic shaman to represent this facet of their wisdom was 'hail'. Unlike rain, hail can damage crops if it comes at a time when they are still in the field. The shaman were experts in the art of weather control, but they also understood that the Earth represented an ecological unity, and that anyone who seriously tampered with that unity was exchanging short-term benefits for long-term disaster. For this reason, the shaman or witch doctors of all primitive cultures will only interfere with climatic conditions after a prolonged spell of one kind of weather — a long dry spell, or a long wet one. They do not arrange the weather on a day-to-day basis. Living in northern climates, the Teutonic shaman also understood that farmers must work within the pattern of the seasons, and that the more closely mankind co-operated with nature, the more successful he would be.

HAGALL therefore represents all events that lie outside the querent's control. These events may be good or bad, but since this Rune indicates the interference of an impersonal force (such as nature, which raineth upon the just and unjust alike) in the querent's life, and since most people react negatively to being treated impersonally, HAGALL most often assumes an unfortunate signification. It is usually taken to represent a disruptive force, and as such refers to those areas of life which cannot be accurately accounted for when planning the future because they do not lie within the querent's jurisdiction. Thus, the events portended by this Rune usually come upon the querent in a sudden and unexpected manner and may constitute a shock or (at the very least) a surprise. Other Runes in the cast, as well as the Rune with which HAGALL is paired, will enable you to assess whether this 'surprise' is likely to be a pleasant or an unpleasant one. Since this Rune is strongly connected with nature and natural happenings, HAGALL sometimes indicates a disruptive natural event, such as sickness, death, a wedding, or a birth. This disruption may or may not cause the querent to abandon his previous course of action, depending on the associated Runes. But in either case, this disruption will last for the whole period covered by the runecast. Thus in a Gate of Heaven runecast, it will refer to the month in which HAGALL appears — or to the whole year if HAGALL is the central Rune. In an Astrological runecast the disruption will last for a full year (or for whatever timespan you have allotted to it). For instance, HAGALL in the Ninth House of an Astrological runecast would indicate that the querent's long distance travel plans would be disrupted for the entire period covered by the reading.

Sometimes HAGALL shows that the querent's future lies in the hands of another person. In some cases, the querent is aware that a decision concerning his future is about to be made, in other cases he is blissfully unaware of what is going on. Because HAGALL is an impersonal Rune, this decision often lies in the hands of a group of people: a board of directors, a county council, a governmental body, a court of law, a tribunal or a committee. Even where the decision appears ultimately to rest with one person, the querent will have little or no personal contact with them, while the person themselves will be acting within a set of rules or conditions which precludes both personal malice and personal favour.

Because the event betokened by HAGALL is accounted an 'act of God' (or of Mother Nature, depending on your point of view) or is the act of some faceless bureaucracy, the querent often learns of it at second hand, through an intermediary or an official letter. Therefore, this rune can indicate the receipt of news, either of some natural event or of some decision taken by a large and influential organization, and this limits personal contact even further.

In an otherwise fortunate runecast, HAGALL can represent an interruption rather than a disruption, following which matters continue much as they did before. This is especially true where HAGALL is paired with a Delay-rune such as IS, NIED or OTHEL reversed. Alternatively, the disruption presaged by HAGALL may cause the querent to change direction completely. As always, much depends on the other Runes in the cast, particularly those following after HAGALL.

Sometimes, the predicted disruption will be fortunate of itself, as when HAGALL indicates a favourable but unexpected decision by government, council, court of justice, or whatever. Or it may bring favourable conditions into the querent's life by deflecting him from an unprofitable or only moderately successful course of action towards a much better one — even though this deflection may be greatly cursed or regretted at the time.

Since all nature's vagaries of climate are ultimately an attempt to reach an ecological balance, and since the tendency of nature is ever towards fertility, the Teutonic shaman saw HAGALL, in one of its aspects, as a Rune of fertility. One of the natural events they saw it presiding over was birth, and it will often signify fertility of mind or body when paired with one of the creativity runes, such as KEN and TIR, or with other fertility runes such as BEORC, LAGU or ING. When such a pairing takes place in the Fifth or Seventh House of an Astrological runecast, the birth is almost always a physical one, and when it takes place in the Third or Ninth House, inspired work is generally betokened.

Because the situations depicted by this Rune may be propitious or the reverse, HAGALL implies that life itself is a gamble. Often, this Rune will appear in a runecast when the querent is taking a big risk which, if it pays off, will result in financial security, emotional fulfilment or repaired health. In this case, the Runes associated with HAGALL will indicate whether the gamble is likely to be successful — though, naturally, much depends on the nature of the risk. HAGALL paired with FEOH or JARA, for instance, would indicate a successful return for hard work and effort invested, but combined with PEORTH it might signify the winning of a lottery, sweepstake or competition. While either FEOH or PEORTH reversed would, of course, signify failure in their respective fields.

HAGALL is a far more complicated rune than any of the other non-reversible Runes. This is because HAGALL is the ninth Rune in the series, and the number nine had a special significance to the Teutonic shaman. You will remember that they believed that there were nine 'worlds' including the one we inhabit, Midgard; and that the twenty-four Universal Forces of the Elder Futhark were formed from various facets or combinations of nine basic energies. All of which makes HAGALL a particularly potent, though enigmatic, symbol.

Divination Practice
The Elemental Cross

Note: For this runecast, WYRD reverts to the meanings explained for it in Chapter 3. It is only in the Asking the Norns runecast that the appearance of the Blank Rune indicates that one should discontinue the reading.

Method
Place the Runes face down on your diviner's cloth, swirl and select five. Lay out the chosen Runes in the order shown in Figure 7.

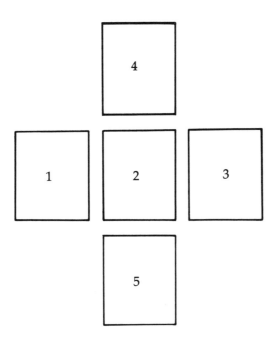

Figure 7: The Elemental Cross

The three horizontal Runes represent the past, present, and future.

The central Rune (position 2) signifies the present. If the querent has a particular problem, the Rune in this position will often indicate what it is. If the Rune is UR, for instance, the querent might be concerned about the consequences of an important and far-reaching change. If it were GEOFU, they would require advice on marital or partnership matters.

Sometimes, however, the Rune in position 2 will represent the querent's state of mind; and since most people consult the Runes when they are in a condition of agitation or distress, it is not unusual to find a negative Rune in this position. Do not let this colour your reading: take it as a clue that your querent is upset, and also as an indication of the immediate cause of their anxiety, but look to the other Runes — particularly those in positions 3, 4 and 5 — in order to ascertain the outcome.

The Rune in position 1 will show what has led to the present state of affairs, and the Rune in position 3 is a Result Rune.

The Rune in position 4 indicates the kind of help the querent can expect. This may come through other people, outside circumstances, or even the querent's own inner resources. Negative Runes here either denote delay, or indicate an unwillingness to accept aid or listen to advice.

The Rune in position 5 indicates what aspects of the situation cannot be altered and must be accepted. Negative Runes in position 5 signify obstacles while positive Runes indicate a lack of opposition and hinderances.

It is a good idea to turn over the central Rune first and decide what the problem is. Then turn over the Rune in position 1 to see what has caused that state of affairs to come into being. Next, examine the three remaining Runes and make a synthesis of their meanings. The future is not immutable: if the querent can come to terms with the limitations of the situation (position 5), and is willing to accept the help or advice offered (position 4), they can often improve on a negative future (position 3).

Finally, look at all the Runes in the cast to see if there is a particular message, or theme, running through them that can be passed on to your querent.

Worked Example
Figure 8 is a runecast for a young woman. The central Rune, WYNN, suggests that she is happy about something. Looking at the Rune in the first position, KEN, we can deduce that this happiness is due to an emotional relationship that has recently come into her life. Since KEN can also represent an offer, we might suppose that it is a proposal that has made her happy. Unless we have strong intuitional prompting in this direction, however, it would be unwise to make this assumption before seeing the other Runes. It may well be that her happiness derives merely from the successful development of a new relationship, and that things have not yet progressed to such a serious level.

In fact, when we turn to the Rune in position 4, we see that she is waiting for the decision of another: the young man has not yet suggested a formal alliance. HAGALL in the sector representing positive factors signifies a

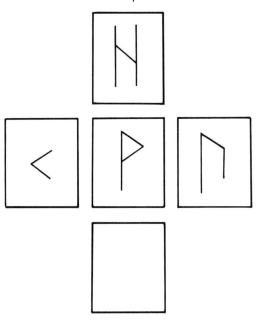

Figure 8: Example of the Elemental Cross Runecast

decision in the querent's favour — or at least, one of which she will approve. And we can tell from the Result Rune, UR, that she is due for a complete change of circumstance which will be wholly to her liking. The Blank Rune falling in position 5 shows that the event will surely come about for it is predestined. She should, therefore, put all her doubts behind her, and await developments with an air of joyful expectation.

Chapter 5

CHOOSING A GEMSTONE

One never-failing source of interest is the subject of 'lucky' gemstones. Anyone taking the trouble to investigate this area of belief will soon find that it is not simply a matter of attributing gems to the signs of the zodiac and leaving it at that. According to ancient esoteric belief, each precious or semi-precious stone had its specific use. The amethyst, for instance, was protection against drunkenness (actually it represents the power to resist the temptation to be intemperate), while the moss agate was said to help in the formation and maintenance of friendships — and of one special friendship in particular — as well as promoting all agricultural or horticultural interests.

There is a veritable treasure house of old lore concerning the use of gemstones to be uncovered through runic divination. There are two methods you can employ in order to find out which gem would be most efficacious for you personally in any particular enterprise. The first is very easy, you just look to the Result Rune in your runecast and take the gem indicated by the symbol found there. This will indicate the stone that will be most helpful to you for that *one purpose only*.

The Teutonic shaman did not believe that there was one all-purpose gemstone that would see us through all the problems that life throws in our paths; there were different stones for different needs, the only exception to this rule being in the case of the Life Reading given on page 176, where the Rune in the central position does indicate a general protective influence. But even this stone may have to be augmented by others on certain occasions where the first stone is out of harmony with the current objective. A gem which vibrates most strongly to the power of love, for example, will be of little use to a person trying to sell a house.

As already mentioned, in a runecast such as the Life Reading where there is no Result Rune, take the Central Rune as indicating which gem you should use. The same injunction holds true for the Astrological runecast given on page 125.

The second method of consulting the Runes to discover your 'lucky' stone for a particular objective is to turn the Runes face down on your diviner's cloth, shuffle them thoroughly and select one. This single Rune will supply the answer.

It makes no difference whether the Rune indicating the gem is upright or reversed, the reversed Rune merely denoting that you could do with a bit of extra luck. Nor should you be alarmed if you select a negative Rune such as NIED, or find one of these *yfelruns* in the Result position of your runecast. In this case, the chances of your wish being fulfilled are not high, but they can be improved by use of the appropriate stone. Remember, all gemstones are useful for something: everything in nature has value, otherwise it would not have come into being. Besides, not all the attributions of gems to Runes are made by correspondence, as will become evident. The catseye, which the Germanic shaman alloted to IS, and Iceland spar, which they ascribed to EOH, are obviously avertive influences; the catseye being a symbol of the Sun which has the power to melt ice; while Iceland spar is a restraining influence on the frenetic energies of Mercury as represented by EOH.

Most of the gemstones used by the Teutonic tribes are well within the scope of the average purse or wallet, and since the fashion for male adornment is on the increase, can be used by either sex.

The moss agate with its dual rulership of friendship and agriculture comes under FEOH. This stone can be found with various bands of colour running through it, and each colour has its own properties. The blue banded variety is good for matters of love and friendship, the types with a green or reddy brown band are helpful for agriculture and animal husbandry, while those with the yellow band are best for people who earn their money by brain-power rather than physical exertion.

To UR is allotted the carbuncle, which has the ability to supply a welcome shot of extra energy just when it is needed. THORN indicates the sapphire, probably as a prophylactic, since Thor's thunderbolts cannot strike out of a sapphire blue sky. The emerald is associated with ANSUR, which may seem unusual for a Mercury-ruled Rune until you remember the Emerald Tablet of Hermes Trismegistus, the Graeco-Egyptian Mercury. RAD's gemstone is the chrysoprase and KEN's is, not surprisingly, the bloodstone.

GEOFU rules the opal, a stone generally held to be unlucky. However, if the Runes indicate that you should wear this gem in order to advance your cause, then you may certainly do so with impunity. The diamond is ascribed to WYNN; little wonder that it is so popular for engagement rings. Don't despair if you feel that you can't afford a diamond, you can substitute the versatile moss agate as your gem as long as you take care to match the colour of the band to your present purpose.

HAGALL is associated with the onyx and NIED with lapis lazuli. The catseye is allocated to IS and the cornelian to JARA. The topaz belongs to YR and the aquamarine to PEORTH, whose smouldering fires are held in check by its gentle, cooling rays. EOLH's gemstone is the amethyst, which represents fidelity and love based on genuine affinity. The ruby, a fiery stone, is under the rulership of SIGEL, while TIR is given charge of coral, a substance more generally associated with Venus than with Mars. I suspect this attribution, in common with several others on the list, was made for allopathic reasons rather than homoeopathic ones.

BEORC is allotted the moonstone, while MANN corresponds to the garnet. Iceland spar is associated with EOH, probably with the intention of giving form and direction to unbridled energy. EOH is the only Rune which has an alternative stone if it is found reversed. This is strange since EOH is the one Rune which doesn't completely alter its meaning when upside down in a cast. The answer is that the energy of EOH is naturally more free-ranging in reverse, in which case it would be a mistake to impose too much discipline on it. When EOH is found in reverse the stone allotted to it is the malachite, but it is still up to the diviner to decide which type, as malachite comes in two varieties: black and white. Do not be held back by any false assumptions about white being 'good' and black being 'evil'. The black malachite will protect you against the dark deeds of others while the white malachite will open new doors or bring relevant knowledge into your hands; so make your choice according to what you need.

The pearl goes with LAGU, while amber is attributed to ING. To DAEG is ascribed the diamond, or the cheaper alternative, the chrysolite, and OTHEL is allocated the ruby. This allocation seems to have been made because of OTHEL's close connections with the sign Capricorn, in which the fiery planet Mars is exalted, or powerful for good.

Lastly, the Blank Rune which has no traditional attribution. Research suggests that it should be associated with a jewelled cuirass sometimes referred to as the Breastplate of Fate or the Breastplate of the Valkyries. But as such an item would be impractical under the conditions of modern life, I suggest the opal as an alternative, the opal being a gemstone having much to do with Fate. Remember that if the Runes advise you to wear this gem then it is quite safe for you to do so. If an individual is following their destiny, then there is no force on earth that can stop them; and an appeal to the Norns, by way of wearing a jewel of Fate, can only strengthen one's position.

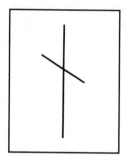

Alternatives	: ╀ ╈ ╊
Letter	: N
Name	: NIED
Meaning	: Necessity
Planetary Rulership	: Saturn (Active)

Saturn was the most distant planet known to the Teutonic astrologers, and due to his shuffling, ponderous circuit of the Zodiac, they personified him in much the same way as we depict Old Father Time. In astrology, the planet Saturn takes many of his attributes from his association with time. For instance, he represents patience, endurance, and caution, all qualities which suggest slow and deliberate action over a relatively long period. NIED, therefore, counsels the querent to have patience, and reminds him of the paradoxical phrase 'to make haste slowly'. It is a Rune which suggests that events will have to work themselves out in their own time, and that no amount of feverish activity will draw them one day nearer.

As we have already seen, Saturn is a teacher, though not always a gentle one, and so NIED signifies all those types of conditions that will develop the attributes of Saturn in the querent's character. Thus, NIED produces delay, constraint, limitation, oppression, affliction, ill-health or lack — which may be lack of vitality, money, or resources. However, unless NIED falls with other negative Runes, it is *not* an indication of failure, especially where the querent is willing to strive patiently towards his goal.

Often, NIED appears as a warning against making changes, particularly where the querent is contemplating throwing in the towel because the odds appear too great or the opposition too strong. It implies that, while the querent is doing all the right things, his problem can only be solved by the passage of time, and though drastic changes are not necessary, patience is, and the querent should adopt a 'wait and see' attitude.

Often, this Rune indicates a long-standing problem or chronic illness (the word *chronic* comes from the Greek word for time, though the expression 'chronic illness' has lost its force because some people use it to mean just a severe illness). With positive Runes, NIED can show that the problem is about to be solved, either in whole or in part; or that the illness will be cured, or at least alleviated, in the near future.

Alternatively, since Saturn signifies limitation and lack, NIED may presage a period of shortage or ill-health. Where there is no long-standing problem or illness, therefore, this Rune acts as a warning to the querent not to take on further duties or responsibilities just at present because, for one reason or another, it is unlikely that he will be able to fulfil or execute them.

In all questions of the type 'should I do such-and-such a thing, or remain as I am?' NIED implies that the querent should stay as they are, since this Rune rules stability and the need to maintain the status quo.

Some runecasters see NIED as the direct equivalent of the modern English word *need*, but this is not entirely correct. I prefer the translation *necessity* because it reminds me that 'necessity is the mother of invention', and NIED always indicates that the querent is passing through a learning situation. Usually, what he is learning is how to develop one of the Saturnian qualities: to have patience, to stick at a job until it is finished, to fulfil all promises or obligations, and to accept set-backs philosophically. However, *need* can be used as a mnemonic too, implying lack or shortage of some kind.

NIED is not a particularly lucky Rune for love affairs, especially where passion is running high, for it is a cold, somewhat dispassionate symbol. Conversely, however, NIED often indicates that the querent is being driven by an emotional need, sometimes — but by no means always — connected with romance. It represents not the fixation, or the fanatical craving which the querent seeks immediately to assuage (although this may also be present) but the tantalizing delay which only serves to inflame desire further.

As a result rune, NIED usually indicates lack of success, unless preceded by very fortunate symbols indeed.

Reversed

In some rune-sets NIED is formed in such a way as to make it impossible to tell whether it is reversed or not. If your rune-set is of this type, you will be forced to use your intuition to distinguish which of the meanings — upright or reversed — is applicable, for there is a difference.

In order to describe the meaning of NIED reversed, it is necessary to say something about the way the Teutonic shaman looked upon evil. They defined it as 'a great force misplaced', and they understood that this misplacement could occur either in time or space. They knew that what is appropriate or conducive to good in one set of circumstances may be inappropriate and give rise only to unhappiness and distress in another.

For this reason, NIED reversed often shows the querent taking an inappropriate or misguided course of action. They may be doing something against the advice of their elders and betters, or against their own conscience, but whatever it is, they are on the road to degradation and ruin for, in reverse, NIED symbolizes inevitable failure leading to hardship, depression and melancholy.

When paired with WYRD or JARA, it often indicates a past mistake for which reparation must now be made. Even when this Rune turns up in an otherwise positive runecast, it signifies that although the querent may make some material gain by his questionable activities, his conscience will give him no peace until he has made amends in some way. This reparation does not always involve restitution or repayment to the person who was originally wronged. On the contrary, this kind of debt is often paid off through suffering in another area of life entirely, or through anguish caused by a third party unconnected with the original misdemeanour. It is a 'comeuppance' — something that is both a punishment for, and a consequence of, the querent's own actions. Sometimes, this Rune signifies that the querent will himself be treated in the same way that he has treated others; while at other times it indicates that the querent will be called upon to pay his debt to society.

Therefore, whenever NIED appears reversed in a runecast, always caution your querent to think twice about any plans he may have in mind. The succeeding Runes in the cast will show how the querent will stand up to this temptation; whether he will conquer it (positive Runes), or if it will conquer him (negative Runes). Where the act has already taken place, this Rune indicates that honesty is the best policy, that the querent should make a clean breast of the situation and attempt to put right any wrong he has done. If the querent does not follow this advice voluntarily, he will be forced to do so by some outside agency — fate (WYRD), an act of God (HAGALL), or human justice (JARA).

Alternatives	: —
Letter	: I
Name	: IS
Meaning	: Ice
Planetary Rulership	: Jupiter (Passive)

As we saw when examining the Rune THORN, Jupiter is a protective planet; ice, too, has the quality of protection or preservation. When we put something 'on ice', we put it into abeyance. According to future developments we may, at a later date, take it 'off ice' and make further use of it — or we may not. The Rune IS has exactly the same significance in a runecast: it indicates that plans must be 'frozen' for the present but may be 'defrosted' again at the appropriate time.

Since IS is one of those Runes which do not appear to reverse themselves, much depends on the other Runes in the cast and on the position of IS itself. In a Result position, this Rune invariably signifies temporary hitches that will soon be sorted out, and its message to the querent is that they should, in the meantime, sit tight and wait for events to take their course. This is also the meaning of IS in any runecast which exhibits a mainly sanguine tone, or where IS is associated with Runes which denote delay rather than total negation of the querent's desires. (THORN, NIED and OTHEL reversed are Delay-runes, while THORN reversed and NIED reversed are particularly associated with the frustration of the querent's hopes.) Depending on the nature of the question and the length of time covered by the runecast, the delay necessitated may be for nine hours, nine days, nine weeks, or nine months.

In a strongly negative runecast, IS suggests that the cooling process has gone too far, and that all enthusiasm and emotion have been chilled out of the situation. It usually indicates that the querent should cut his losses and move on to a more stimulating project or a more productive relationship.

Because ice is the enemy of warmth, it is in the area of love and friendship that IS is at its most unhelpful. By their very nature, relationships are difficult to rekindle once they have been subjected to coldness, and this Rune often shows a cooling off of enthusiasm in emotional or career matters. In questions concerning love, IS generally indicates a separation, often combined with ill-feeling and resentment. Love, in this context, also covers family and close friendships — anyone from whom the querent would normally expect loyalty and support. In questions in which relationships play a prominent part, the problem often revolves around a breach of loyalty, sometimes on the part of the querent, but more often on the part of the other person involved.

However, in questions concerning the implementation of a plan or the achievement of some goal, the effects of this Rune are not nearly so detrimental, and the usual meaning of 'delay' can be applied.

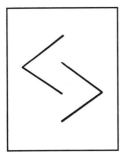

Alternatives	: ◇ ♦ ⑤ ⑸ ⅃
Letter	: J
Name	: JARA
Meaning	: Harvest
Planetary Rulership	: Mercury (Neutral)

Odin, who is the equivalent of Mercury in the Norse/Germanic system, was the god of the dead, the overlord of Valhallah where the noblest and strongest warriors went after death. Valhallah means 'the Hall of the Chosen', and like the Christian concept of Heaven, the idea behind it is one of recompense or reward. The Rune JARA refers to this aspect of Odin's power and is, therefore, concerned with rewarding the querent for his previous actions. Because Odin chose only the noblest of warriors to go to Valhallah, Jara is a Rune much associated with justice and, by analogy, all legal matters come under its auspices.

The word 'jara' does not exactly mean 'year' as it is often translated, but 'time of year' — the time of year specifically referred to being harvest time. This is why I have given JARA the meaning of *harvest*, rather than *year*. Its appearance in a runecast signifies that the querent will be reaping a reward for efforts expended, a repayment in money or in kind for previous outlay.

It is often hard to judge JARA — like all Runes that do not show a positive or a negative face. Sometimes it will fall in a prominent position in a runecast, such as the placement indicating the Problem, to denote that the querent is concerned about a legal matter of some kind. However, the appearance of JARA does not necessarily show that the judgement will go in the querent's favour — just as GEOFU appearing in a cast indicates only that the querent is concerned about their love-life without being of itself any indication as to how matters will progress.

When JARA falls in a Result Position, it generally takes a positive connotation, unless the Runes associated with it are extremely unfortunate. In this position it indicates a successful gathering in, a just return for invested effort and the reaping of a well-earned reward. In a negative runecast, JARA in the Result Position suggests that the failure intimated by the accompanying Runes could be prevented, in whole or in part, by greater application on the part of the querent.

Paired with HAGALL, NIED or WYRD, JARA often indicates that the querent is attempting to follow a path in life to which they are not suited, and that they are tempting fate by so doing. JARA is obviously a double-edged Rune, signifying 'as ye sow, so shall ye reap'.

Because it embodies the concept of justice, JARA often appears in a runecast to indicate legal or judicial matters — even where the problem will never actually go to Court. It can, therefore, have reference to all legal contracts, or documents such as leases or contracts of employment. It can also indicate wills and, by extension, the legalities attached to them. Sometimes it represents the abstract quality of legal advice (especially when paired with ANSUR or MANN) and is then taken to represent the lawyer or solicitor concerned. But it can indicate anyone called upon to make a judgement in a professional capacity, such as a doctor or bank manager.

Since marriage is also a contract, it is possible for JARA to signify marriage. By the same token, though, and when associated with adverse Runes, it can indicate the dissolution of the marriage-contract with all the attendant legal complications entailed.

Because JARA signifies a specific time of year, it implies that the events denoted by the Runes associated with it must come to fruition in their own time and cannot be rushed. For this reason, it often indicates a hiatus period while legal complications are sorted out or before contracts can be signed or exchanged. This is particularly the case when NIED also holds a prominent place in the runecast.

Some manuals on runic divination give JARA the time indication of 'in one year' on the grounds that JARA is supposed to mean 'a year'; but in my experience it usually signifies a period in late September or early October — the time of year at which Europe celebrates the Harvest Festival — just as FEOH signifies the month of May, which the Anglo-Saxons called 'Trimilci' — 'three milkings' — because at that time of the year the cattle, gorging themselves on the new grass, needed to be milked three times a day.

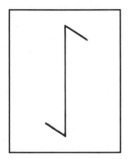

Alternatives	: —
Letter	: Y
Name	: YR
Meaning	: A Yew Tree
Planetary Rulerships	: Jupiter and the South Node

YR has several different names in various Norse and Germanic dialects, but behind them all is the one unwavering concept of defence against danger. Since the two meanings allotted to this Rune for the purposes of divination are both closely associated with the yew tree, I prefer to use the name YR, which means a yew tree.

Yew was the best wood for the manufacture of long-bows, and for centuries the long-bow was the Englishman's prime defence. Jupiter, one of the rulers of YR, is a protective planet, as we have already seen. He is also the ruler of Sagittarius, the sign of the Archer. Thus, one of the meanings allotted to YR is taken directly from the vocabulary of toxophily, for it is said to indicate that the querent has his sights set on a viable target, one well within the compass of his abilities to achieve and that, for this reason, nothing is likely to stand in the way of the querent's success.

Yew itself is an avertive wood and was, in earlier times, a churchyard tree symbolic of resurrection. No matter how bad things seem, when YR holds a significant place in a runecast it indicates that the situation will leap back into life again and turn in the querent's favour.

YR's second meaning is connected with its secondary planetary ruler, the Moon's South Node. In Teutonic mythology, this invisible point on the Moon's orbit was associated with the two wolves who were supposed to pursue the Sun and the Moon, endeavouring to swallow them. Whenever there was a Solar or Lunar eclipse (which can only take place when both the Sun and the Moon are in alignment with the North and South Nodes) the Teutons would say that one of these wolves had caught and swallowed the luminary concerned. This was a very dangerous time, and is still accounted so in modern astrology; but soon the wolf would be forced by Thor (the Norse equivalent of Jupiter) to disgorge its prize, and the danger would pass. Thus, the second meaning of YR is: a hindrance or minor catastrophe which either never fully materializes or turns out in the end to have been to the querent's advantage.

The Runes following YR in the cast — especially the Rune in the Result Position, if there is one — will indicate which of these two interpretations is likely to apply.

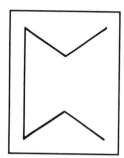

Alternatives	: ᛔ ᛈ ᚹ
Letter	: P
Name	: PEORTH
Meaning	: A Dice Cup
Planetary Rulership	: Mars and the South Node

Whereas with YR there have been several words used to describe the single concept embodied in the runic symbol, with PEORTH we have no clear indication philologically speaking of what root idea this Rune is intended to represent, for the exact interpretation of PEORTH has not come down to us. It has been variously translated as a *hearth* or a *chessman* (on the evidence of Runic Poems, all of which are too late to be reliable) or the translation I have adopted here — a dice cup. My own researches indicate that, of all the suggestions offered, this latter is the most apposite — particularly if the habits of the early Teutons are taken into account.

They used dice made of animal bone — not for gaming, but for divination. The simple casting of lots was an easy and uncomplicated way of looking into the future, and it was much favoured by the Teutonic armies — which gives us a connection with the Rune's planetary ruler, Mars. War is a risky business, and a soldier may meet his death in any battle in which he participates. Little wonder that fighting men of all nations have always been interested in drawing back the veil from the unrevealed future. The Roman legionnaires cast lots — and so, according to Homer, did the Greeks at the seige of Troy, where they used pebbles in a helmet rather than dice.

The event signified by the number on the dice thrown from the dice cup, or by the pebble which jumped out of the helmet, was not felt to have fallen by *chance* in the sense that the modern, scientific mind understands the word. *Chance* was an aspect of WYRD, the Three Norns, or Fates. The Romans called the goddess of fate Fortuna, the goddess of Fortune, and we still use the term 'fortune teller' to mean someone who can reveal to us our fate. Modern gamblers call her 'Lady Luck' — and believe in her as firmly as any pagan ever did.

PEORTH's meaning in a runecast is connected to this idea of the disclosure of something previously unrevealed because it indicates that something hidden will come to light. Generally speaking, it is a fortunate omen. Sometimes the querent will recover a lost article; sometimes they will be offered a second chance in a relationship or in their career; sometimes it shows the querent taking up an opportunity which was previously ignored or overlooked.

With negative Runes, or in the Sixth House of an Astrological runecast, it may foretell the outbreak of an illness. Other Runes in the cast will show how the malady is likely to proceed. In matters of sickness, however, PEORTH often indicates an illness which does not yield to normal medical treatment, but is more susceptible to homoeopathy, or naturopathy or to occult or magical methods such as acupuncture, aromatherapy, psychic healing and hypnotism.

PEORTH can refer to any secret the querent is trying to keep. And since most people only attempt to suppress facts about themselves that they would be embarrassed to have made public, more often than not it refers to a *guilty* secret. It can, however, refer to anything the querent feels shy or reticent about — or that he would rather not discuss with the reader. This need not be anything evil or wrong, just some area about which the querent is sensitive, so it is usually best not to make any judgements on this score.

Another secret matter — inasmuch as it is essentially a private thing between two people — is sex. This Rune regularly appears in conjunction with other emotionally oriented Runes (KEN, TIR, UR, GEOFU, WYNN, BEORC and LAGU), to indicate that a couple are sexually compatible. Mars, the planetary ruler of PEORTH, is a significator of passion, and when this Rune falls in the Fifth, Seventh, or Twelfth House of an Astrological runecast without being paired by one of these emotional Runes, or in conjunction with UR reversed, KEN reversed, or TIR reversed, it can indicate a relationship based solely on sexual attraction and thus fated to burn itself out if no other point of contact can be established.

A person who speculates about the future is one who tries to guess or anticipate coming events; but in English 'a speculator' is also a gambler, whether they inhabit the relatively respectable world of property and stocks and shares or the less professional sphere of horse-racing, football pools and bingo. This ties in with PEORTH's meaning, 'a dice cup', and this Rune also indicates the successful guessing or intuiting of the result of a game of chance, or chancy event. For this reason, PEORTH often represents an unearned gain of money — especially in association with HAGALL, since that Rune has the significance of 'a decision or final outcome in the hands of another'. In this case 'another' is WYRD, Fortuna, Lady Luck.

Since a legacy cannot truly be said to be earned, PEORTH falling with legacy Runes like JARA and OTHEL can indicate an inheritance. This links with PEORTH's other meaning — 'secrecy' — since what happens after death remains shrouded in mystery for the majority of people.

Sometimes this Rune will indicate a gift of money rather than a win or an inheritance. The motives for such a gift should be examined with great care by the querent, since PEORTH's association with secrecy and sexuality often points to unsuspected strings of an emotional or sexual nature being attached to the arrangement.

Since things which are secret are unrevealed (or only revealed to the chosen) PEORTH has much to do with the occult, which itself means 'hidden'. For this reason it will occasionally signify that a querent has occult or mediumistic powers; i.e. powers that will enable them to contact that shadowy world known as the Astral Light, some of whose inhabitants are Elemental Spirits, while yet others are the shades of the dead.

Reversed

When PEORTH is upright, the secret or hidden things which come to light are generally of a pleasant or fortuitous nature. In reverse, however, PEORTH tends to unearth unpleasant surprises and uncover the darker deeds that others have perpetrated against us. Because of this, PEORTH reversed often heralds a disappointment — and the querent may be let down either by circumstances or by another person, often a close friend. Though this Rune may occasionally act as a symbol of betrayal in love or friendship, when found reversed the disappointment more often tends to centre on financial loss. The querent should, therefore, be advised not to invest money during the period covered by the reading. Since PEORTH reversed is also connected with disloyalty, the querent should not lend money either — particularly to a friend — during the period indicated, as it will probably not be repaid or will be regained only after much difficulty. Nor does this Rune denote a good time for gambling when it is reversed. Lady Luck is not smiling upon the querent at this time; and his hunches — however strong — are not likely to prove correct.

In short, when PEORTH appears reversed in a runecast, we can say that events will not turn out as well as the querent had hoped.

Since its upright position can denote sexual compatibility, the reversal of PEORTH can denote sexual disharmony and incompatibility. With Runes indicative of waning enthusiasm (IS and all Mars-ruled Runes in reverse — UR, KEN and TIR) it shows that one partner no longer finds the other physically attractive, while the other partner continues to be sexually demanding. How this state of affairs will eventually work out can be judged from the succeeding Runes in the cast.

Because of its connection with the occult, PEORTH reversed can signify uninformed experimentation with spiritualism or altered states of consciousness which will provide the querent with rather more excitement than they had bargained for — such as disturbing psychic manifestations subsequent to the use of a Ouija Board as an after-dinner entertainment!

As the purely visual side of the Astral experiences obtained through magical training can also be achieved by the use of narcotics, PEORTH reversed sometimes indicates an involvement with drugs — usually a debilitating one.

In questions touching upon emotional matters, PEORTH reversed in the First or Seventh House of an Astrological runecast often shows that there is a sexual problem of some kind lurking in the background. In the First House, the problem is the querent's; in the Seventh House, their partner's. It can indicate one or other of those activities that society looks upon as perverted — sadism, masochism, tranvestism and the like.

Either way up, PEORTH in the First House paired with ANSUR reversed will often indicate that you are reading for a male homosexual, and when paired with LAGU reversed, that you are reading for a lesbian (always depending, of course, on the sex of your querent); while the pairing of PEORTH either way up with RAD upright or reversed usually indicates that the querent is ambivalent in their sexuality.

I must stress, however, that these observations would apply *only* where the question put by the querent relates directly to their love life. In other areas of experience — especially those revolving around money or career — these combinations would have to be read quite differently.

Divination Practice
Mimir's Head

Mimir's Head is an answering runecast. It is not necessary that the querent should tell the reader what the question is, though while you are still feeling your way, you may prefer that they verbalize their problem rather than keep it to themselves. Nor is one limited only to 'Yes or No' questions. One can ask questions like: 'How will things turn out if...?' or 'What should I do about...?'

This runecast is similar to the preceding one, but it gives more details concerning the background to the problem, and also includes a section on advice. In fact, it derives its name from the oracular head of the god Mimir, which Odin himself consulted in times of trouble. Runic advice is generally of a positive tone, and will usually take the attitude that, if you can't get over a problem, you should go round it. So, even where the Runes in positions 5 and 6 are negative you should examine them carefully in order to assess what positive comment you can make. With NEID reversed in either of these positions, for instance, you might have to advise the querent not to go through with a particular scheme, but you could also tell them that they were displaying a very negative attitude — materialistic, cynical, pessimistic — which it would be well for them to revise.

Timing
Normally, this runecast will read up to three months into the past and the same distance into the future, but a lot depends on the type of question asked. A 'mixed' answer that you genuinely cannot make head or tail of will sometimes indicate 'Yes, but not within three months'. A different type of runecast (the Gate of Heaven, or one of the Astrological runecasts, for instance) will often give a clearer picture.

Method
Place the Runes face downwards on your diviner's cloth. Swirl and select seven, which should be laid out as shown in Figure 9.

Read the first two Runes as a pair. These represent the problem. Reading Runes in pairs is an important feature of many runecasts, and time devoted to mastering the knack will be well spent. Try to combine the meanings, or consider what the two Runes have in common. Are they, for instance, both Delay-runes, signifying a waiting period? Or both Fertility-runes, indicating increase or gain for the querent? You will usually find that each Rune illuminates the meaning of the other in some way even where one is positive and the other negative. But reading Runes in pairs *is* a knack, so do not be disheartened if you are unable to do it straight off.

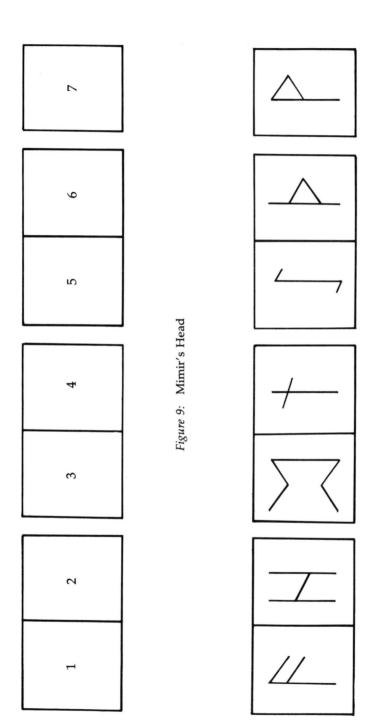

Figure 9: Mimir's Head

Figure 10: Example of Mimir's Head Runecast

In the example in Figure 10, ANSUR is coupled with HAGALL. The querent is probably worried about some exam results, since ANSUR indicates a test of some kind and HAGALL represents an impersonal decision concerning the enquirer.

Next, read Runes 3 and 4 as a pair. These show the outside factors which have led to the present position. Sometimes these factors are helpful, and sometimes they are not. As with the previous runecast, the Elemental Cross, Runes 1 and 2 occasionally show the problem as the querent sees it, while Runes 3 and 4 shed a more objective light on the matter.

Continuing our example of the anxious student, we find PEORTH reversed and NIED in positions 3 and 4, indicating that a recent disappointment in love or friendship (PEORTH reversed) has thrown him into a state of depression, which has weakened his concentration and interfered with his studies (NIED).

Now the third pair of Runes can be read. These are the kernel of the runecast, and represent the advice given by the runic powers as to how the problem should be handled. They may advise a particular course of action; they may suggest a shift of emphasis; or they may indicate that the best thing to do is to 'lie low and say nuffin''.

Our student, for example, has drawn YR and THORN in positions 5 and 6. These are both Delay-runes — which is only to be expected, since he must wait for his papers to be marked — but, equally, both indicate good fortune at the end of the waiting period. This would suggest that things are not as bad as they seem. The querent's depressed state of mind is encouraging him to look on the black side when, in actuality, he has been more successful than he imagines.

The seventh and final position represents the result. However, this Rune should not be read in isolation, but in the light of the rest of the reading. For, although a positive Rune indicates a positive answer, it will only do so insofar as the Result Rune is in harmony with the matter enquired about. (A man with no business partners, asking a purely business question, is not going to be thrilled if he is told at the end of a disastrous reading that his marriage is going to be strengthened by adversity because GEOFU falls in the final place.) NIED in this position, for instance, may mean 'no' in a reading of negative tone and 'yes, but not yet', in a more positive one.

In our example, the answer is quite straightforward. WYNN signifies success of hopes, particularly with regard to career prospects. Our student will gain his 'pass', and has every chance of landing the kind of job he desires.

Chapter 6

FLOWERS AND THE RUNES

No less fascinating than the runic lore of precious and semi-precious stones is the connection between the Runes and growing things. There was a runic herbal lore and a tree lore, as well as a flower lore and an agricultural lore. For reasons given in the section relating to SIGEL, this book is not concerned with the runic aspect of herbalism. However, many people are interested in gardening and for them I include a list of flower allocations.

Either the appropriate Rune may be extracted from your runeset and carried with you when planting or bedding out your blooms, which will help them to grow strong and healthy; or you may choose a flower to help you with a particular aim in exactly the same way that you would choose a gemstone, by reference to the Result Rune in a cast or by specifically selecting a runic symbol, and use the corresponding plant to decorate the home, to wear or to give as a present. Although I have not given any details about healing and diagnosis by the Runes, I have found that the gift of a bunch of flowers or a pot plant of the variety indicated by the Runes has a wonderful effect on the morale of an ailing person. In fact, floral magic works best in the areas of health and domestic problems, probably because plants, by their earthy natures and delicate colourings, suggest the twin virtues of stability and harmony. They are also excellent at helping love affairs along and revitalizing marriages that have lost their 'sparkle'.

The flower associated with FEOH is the lily of the valley, a hardy plant which will grow virtually anywhere. The nasturtium belongs to UR, and honesty is attributed to THORN, which is not unusual since the god Thor had much to do with the concept of justice, and oaths were often sworn on Thor's hammer. ANSUR rules the morning glory, while RAD's flower is the snapdragon. For KEN you are given a choice: gorse or the wild rose. Either is acceptable, so make your decision according to the season and the availability of the plant concerned. Lad's love is the flower of GEOFU while for WYNN, if your problem is an emotional/sexual one, you should use love-in-a-mist, otherwise settle for larkspur.

HAGALL rules ferns and also all plants that cannot be grown in northern climates except under artificial conditions, such as orchids, or anything grown out of season. NIED is allotted the humble crocus that prospers in the most negative conditions, and IS has dominion over the heliotrope (for money matters) and the sweet pea (for all matters of relationships and dealing with other people). IS also rules a group of magical plants including Solomon's seal and the sorcerer's periwinkle, but their use is a specialist subject all on its own which, however interesting it may seem, the beginner should leave severely alone.

Cornflowers are the plants of JARA, since corn (harvest) and cornflowers go together. YR rules lilac and PEORTH is associated with the chrysanthemum. One of the names given to the Rune EOLH means 'sedge', so it is not surprising that the plant of EOLH is the rush. St John's wort is attributed to SIGEL and the red hot poker to TIR. BEORC rules the moonflower and MANN guards the foxglove. The foxglove provides a drug which is good for the heart, and 'heart' is often a synonym for a humane attitude, as in the expression 'have a heart'.

EOH is associated with forsythia and LAGU with waterlilies or, if these are not available, night scented stock. Night scented stock may also be used as a substitute for BEORC's moonflowers, which are something of a rarity these days. The gentian is allocated to ING, the marigold or cowslip to DAEG, and the snowdrop to OTHEL, this latter for the same reason as the crocus is given to NIED.

As with the gems, there is no traditional association for the Blank Rune. The mystical vibrations of the purple iris, however, will enable the aspiring runic shaman to co-operate with his or her allotted destiny should the Blank Rune be drawn as an indicator.

It is customary, when picking flowers or herbs for magical purposes, to explain what you are doing to the Spirit of the Land — usually a localized form of the goddess Freyja. This can be said out loud, or if this embarrasses you, formulated in the mind. But it should be done whether you are in your own garden or in the depths of the country. It is really a plea to the forces of nature not so much to allow you to gather the plant in question (since you intend to do that anyway) as to permit *virtue* to remain in the plant after cutting. If the nature deities do not consent to do this, your flowers will lack efficacy. This is an important point often overlooked these days. It is also worth remembering that, so long as the Runes have indicated that a certain flower could be of help to you, it is highly unlikely that the Earth Spirits will refuse your request. However, you *must* make the request as the nature gods do not like to be taken for granted.

Pick or cut only what you need, and always be careful to leave two or three of the flowers you are collecting — blooms or individual plants, depending on the species — still growing.

It is of little moment that some of these plants were unknown to the early Teutons: the principle behind the allocations remains the same. This can best be seen in the attributions of HAGALL where the shaman is able to choose any plant alien to their own part of the world or grown under artificial conditions. The same sort of reasoning could be applied to flowers associated with FEOH where almost any hardy shrub would be applicable; and so on right through the list.

In my opinion too much attention is paid to out-of-date tables of correspondences and not enough to attempting to understand the timeless principles which led to those correspondences being made in the first place. Of course, runic magic of the twentieth century is not the same as the runic magic practised in the pre-Christian era, but why should we want it to be? The world has moved on and so has occult science, and it is a mistake to waste time mourning for the past when so much needs to be done in the present. Our methods of agriculture, manufacture and warfare are all different from the old Norse and Anglo-Saxon way of doing things, so why shouldn't this apply to magic too?

The foregoing remarks apply equally to the allocation of gemstones, though since the Vikings were great travellers whose traces have been discovered from Byzantium to the Americas, it is probable that all the jewels and minerals mentioned in Chapter 5 were known to the peoples of the North by the commencement of the Christian age.

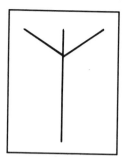

Alternatives   : Ψ
Letter   : Z
Name   : EOLH
Meaning   : An Elk
Planetary Rulerships : Jupiter and Venus

Here is another Rune whose name is in dispute. Unlike PEORTH, where philologists have no clear idea what the name means, the problem with EOLH is that it has had several names — but all with different meanings (see Chapter 1). An examination of these names, however, reveals that they all relate to the same nexus of ideas — the main difficulty being that unless one understands the Teutonic mentality the connections remain mystifying.

Perhaps the easiest way for the modern mind to come at the solution to this problem is via the astrological correspondences allotted to EOLH. The planet Venus was called the Lesser Benefic in medieval astrology, while Jupiter was called the Greater Benefic; so the main idea conveyed is of good fortune of some kind coming to the querent. In fact, this Rune signifies a fortunate new influence entering the querent's life. This comes about, very often, not through a logical or conscious process of thought, but largely through the unconscious promptings of the emotions or instincts. The new influence may be a stimulating and absorbing hobby, or a new job or career change that will involve the querent in study. Or it can be a new relationship with a person who is kindhearted, generous, and of an outgoing disposition. EOLH is a Rune of friendship, and so this new relationship could be with a person of either sex. Where backed by other Love-runes, however, EOLH can signify a romance based on friendship and trust.

The fact that the meaning of EOLH is an Elk — which, along with the reindeer, was the main source of food for the more northerly Teutons — may seem to belie these interpretations; but hunting and farming communities think differently to us about the slaughter of animals, and their relationship with animals was very different to our own. We can tell from the magical rites — as depicted in rock paintings and carvings — that these people believed that the animals killed in a hunt were delivered into their hands by the gods. At the highest level, they believed that the animal gave up its life so that mankind might live. One of the meanings of EOLH, therefore, is 'sacrifice' — but it is important to remember that the sacrifice must be a willing one. In formal sacrifice, the beast that pulled away from the altar or struggled under the knife was an unfortunate augury. Likewise, the Berserkers (see page 92) went cheerfully into battle, accepting that, if they were to die, they would do so as a sacrifice to Odin. EOLH, therefore, indicates a joyous exchange of a lesser good for a greater.

Beryl Mercer (on the authority of Sid Birchby) names this Rune Eolhx which means 'heal-pebble', i.e. amber; and this emphasizes another aspect of this symbol, namely: protection.

Freya's necklace, Brisingamen, was made of amber, and was the feminine equivalent of the masculine hammer of Thor. It acted as an inner protection within the walls of Asgard, ensuring peace and harmony at the Council of the Aesir, as the northern gods were called, just as the hammer was used to smite the frost-giants and other enemies of the gods. Thus EOLH's appearance in a runecast is often a protective sign, like the appearance of the other Jupiter-ruled Runes THORN and YR. It indicates that the querent is shielded from harm in all that he does during the period covered by the reading. If anything does start to go wrong, the querent often receives a strong premonition of disaster which comes with such startling force and clarity that it cannot be ignored.

So beneficial is this Rune that it has become the symbol of well-founded optimism, and when it falls in the First House of an Astrological runecast, it signifies that the querent has great confidence in himself and his abilities, coupled with a tremendous faith in the future.

Reversed
The keynote of EOLH reversed is vulnerability. In reverse, the negative aspect of sacrifice is brought into play, for then this Rune signifies that others are only too willing to sacrifice the querent's future prospects to ensure their own success. The querent will be made the victim of other people's schemes and machinations unless great care is taken. Often, EOLH depicts the querent being used, or taken advantage of in emotional or business affairs, or being made the scapegoat for other people's errors.

Wherever the question relates to matters of love, friendship or business, the querent should beware of rushing into any new relationship until he knows a little more about the other person's character.

Usually, EOLH indicates that the querent will be deceived by others; but sometimes it shows that the querent is himself suffering from misapprehensions about a situation, or has over-optimistically misread the intentions of others. This Rune in reverse — particularly in the First House of an Astrological runecast — often signifies that the querent is the sort of person who expects something for nothing (no outlay, no effort, and so on) and is thus ripe for being both conned and disappointed. Even where active deception by others is concerned, this type of mentality is always willing to meet the deceiver half way. For this reason, EOLH reversed is often a sign of an unsuccessful business venture or financial deal — one built on the shifting sand of the querent's own naïvety, greed, and gullibility.

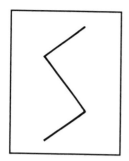

Alternatives	: ᛌᛁᛁᛉ
Letter	: S
Name	: SIGEL
Meaning	: The Sun
Planetary Rulership	: The Sun

There is a happy agreement between the name of this Rune and its planetary ruler, since both signify the Sun. Unfortunately, there is little in either Norse or Germanic legend to indicate exactly what place the Sun held in Scandinavian or Teutonic theology.* The one recurrent theme, however, is that the rising Sun could turn the evil Frost Giants into stone — which is another way of saying that he struck them 'stone dead'. Tolkein — himself a scholar of Anglo-Saxon — reworked this concept in the episode of the squabbling Trolls in *The Hobbit*.

In one form or another, this ability to vanquish evil is almost universally awarded to the Sun. In Latin, for instance, one of the Sun's titles is 'Invictor', because in any battle between Light and Darkness the Sun will always be victorious. SIGIL, therefore, is a Rune of victory, and its appearance in a runecast is a promise of success and achievement. It also denotes that any opposition the querent may be experiencing at the time of the reading is certain to be well and truly routed. It is particularly fortunate to have this Rune in the result position in a runecast since it generally indicates that, since a successful resolution of the problem is assured, the querent can afford to relax a little and let events take their course.

When surrounded by Business-Runes like RAD or WYNN, and Material-Runes like NIED, OTHEL and — sometimes — FEOH, SIGEL frequently

---

* Some English speaking researchers have been misled into thinking that the ancient Teutons thought of the Sun as representing the feminine principle in nature and the Moon as representing the masculine principle. This has occurred because the word for Sun in German and related languages is feminine while the word for Moon is masculine, but in those languages in which common nouns possess gender, there are all sorts of anomalies between the sex of a thing, real or assumed, and the gender imposed upon it linguistically.

I will not deny that the situation as regards the Sun and the Moon is confused by the presence in the Germanic/Scandinavian pantheon of a primitive Moon god, Manni. However, many cultures had Moon gods co-existing side by side with Moon goddesses. Sin is a Moon god, Khonsu is a Moon god, and so (to a certain extent) is Thoth, as the crescent Moon he wears on his head bears witness. Invariably this Moon god is a deity presiding over ritual magic and formal divination, while the goddess aspect deals, Circe-like, with enchantment, fascination and clairvoyance.

signifies that the querent is a workaholic. The personality type depicted by this Rune cannot slow down. They do, however, have the capacity to play as hard as they work, and it is often worth suggesting that they learn to redirect some of their energy into recreational pursuits. For this type of person, a change is as good as — and frequently much better than — a rest.

The majority of people who consult the Runes do so because they have something on their minds. Thus, SIGEL regularly turns up in a runecast to indicate that the tension and worry occasioned by the querent's difficulties have begun to take their toll. When this is the case, SIGEL intimates that the querent has become run down or otherwise drained of nervous energy, but that a little rest and relaxation are probably all that is needed to restore equilibrium.

Sometimes, when paired with negative Runes, SIGEL reveals that the querent has a tendency to fret endlessly over their problems while at the same time experiencing a reluctance to do anything about them; but it is more usual in this situation for SIGEL to indicate that the querent is the sort of person who wants to be the sole arbiter of their own fate, the centre of their own world just as the sun is the centre of our Solar System; and where circumstances will not allow this to be the case, the querent becomes distressed and anxious in consequence. Accompanying Runes to watch out for in this context are Fate-Runes and Delay-Runes, such as WYRD, HAGALL, NIED, THORN or IS. The most troublesome of these is NIED, which is the natural antithesis of SIGEL, being both a Fate-Rune and a Delay-Rune.

In common with other ancient philosophers, the Teutonic shaman saw the sun as being the symbol of the life force, the root of vitality in all living things, including mankind. SIGEL is thus a Rune of health, usually signifying abundant energy and strength coupled with a positive mental outlook. However, as we have seen with other Runes which do not have a reversed meaning, SIGEL may sometimes appear in the position indicative of the present (or the problem), merely to indicate that the querent is concerned about their health. As with the previous examples of this type, it is the other Runes in the cast that will reveal whether there is any basis for concern, and if there is, how the illness is likely to progress.

There is an aspect of runic divination that deals with diagnosis and prognosis, but it is not an area into which novices should allow themselves to be drawn since, in inexperienced hands, it can do more harm than good. For this reason, I have made no attempt to explain the mechanics of runic diagnosis in this book.

In all questions relating to health matters, I would suggest that you content yourself with looking only at the general trend of the reading. Positive runes — especially those relating to the flow of the life force (such as KEN and TIR) or to the restoration of balance between mind and body (like GEOFU, DAEG and ING) indicate that the querent possesses strong natural powers of recuperation and resistance. Often, under these circumstances, the body rapidly throws off the illness, causing the patient the minimum of debility and discomfort.

Where the runecast consists of a mixture of negative and positive Runes —
and particularly where a negative Rune occupies the Result Position — you
should advise the querent to take their problem to a doctor. It is amazing how
many people — suspecting that they might have something wrong with them
— are willing to consult anybody and everybody about their symptoms *except* a
qualified medical practitioner. Try not to alarm your querent. Simply point out
that it is the doctor's job to cure — or at least alleviate — our ills. In this respect,
it is useful to note that ANSUR, JARA or MANN in association with SIGEL
signifies that a correct diagnosis will facilitate a speedy recovery. Also, the
Runes GEOFU, DAEG and ING are illustrative of a burden being lifted from
the querent's mind as a result of growing confidence — either in the ability of
the doctor or the efficacy of the treatment prescribed.

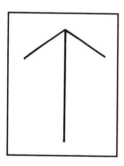

Alternatives	: T 1
Letter	: T
Name	: TIR
Meaning	: The God Tir
Planetary Rulership	: Mars (Active)

Tir is one of the oldest of the Teutonic deities, and in the distant past may even
have outranked Odin as leader of the gods. His name is pronounced
differently in many dialects — Tyr, Zio, Zivis — but to the Anglo-Saxons he
was TIW, from which we derive the word 'Tuesday' (literally: Tiw's day). Like
Mars, his Roman counterpart, Tir was a war god, and the Rune which bears
his name therefore represents victory in battle, or victory in any situation in
which there is an element of contest or competition. Thus TIR may signify the
competitive nature of most business activities, as well as those forms of
selection which arrive at their conclusions by comparing the promise or
performance of the participants — as happens in sport, examinations,
interviews and tenders for work.

To the ancient Teutons, TIR was the soldier's Rune, and was used as a
talisman by the Berserkers — the crack fighting troops of the Norse and
Icelandic tribes who gave their name to a particular form of destructive
madness. This came about because the Berserkers quite literally *went mad* in
the heat of battle. As Dion Fortune says in her essay 'God and the Gods',* the
Mars force is one of the easiest to invoke, and one of the hardest to control.
Even when the querent is not normally competitive, the appearance of TIR in a

* Dion Fortune's *Applied Magic and Aspects of Occultism* (The Aquarian Press, 1987).

prominent place in a runecast indicates that this aspect of their character has been activated — that they have 'seen red' (a notoriously Martian colour), and are determined not to be bested. Sometimes, this feeling arises from a sense of being goaded, dared or thwarted by another person or by circumstances — or it may be occasioned by an overwhelming feeling of enthusiasm for the matter in hand.

TIR is a Rune of *motivation*. It signifies strength of will and a competitive spirit allied to a single-minded involvement with a project or an ideal which systematically breaks down all barriers that threaten its successful completion. Because most wars are fought for conquest or gain, TIR usually indicates either an increase of power or an increase in wealth — sometimes both. When well placed in a runecast, TIR represents the querent rising in the world — or in the estimation of others — through their own efforts.

Of course, not all wars are fought for material conquest. Some are holy wars, such as the Jihads and the Crusades. For this reason, TIR can sometimes indicate that the querent has taken up some kind of cause which they are pursuing with missionary zeal. The cause itself might be a personal or humanitarian one, but in either case the querent generally sees themselves as fighting for right against the forces of evil and oppression — for TIR is the Rune of the reformer, the campaigner, the activist, the militant. It represents those who are prepared to fight — metaphorically or in reality — to ensure the triumph of what they see as justice and fair play.

Because TIR represents rising enthusiasm, much depends on the Runes which follow it in a runecast. Positive Runes — especially Success-Runes like FEOH, YR and SIGEL — indicate that the querent will go from strength to strength; but negative Runes will show that although the querent may be angry and determined to 'get even' or rectify an injustice, the opposition will prove too strong for them in the end.

In the days of hand-to-hand fighting, most warriors sustained wounds at one time or another. Indeed, old soldiers were always proud to show off their battle scars. Thus TIR also has the meaning: 'you will live to fight again another day', and for this reason it is particularly lucky for TIR to fall upright in a runecast when the querent is expecting to undergo surgery because it then indicates a successful operation followed by a rapid convalescence.

When reading for a male querent, TIR will often represent the querent himself, and much can be surmised about his outlook concerning his present situation from the upright or reversed position of the Rune. Upright, it indicates physical stamina and moral strength. Often, the querent suspects that he is going to have to fight for his rights, or in order to get what he wants, but is nevertheless confident of success. As with FEOH, which also signifies victory despite opposition, it is not unusual to find TIR paired with a negative Rune indicative of obstacles, anxiety or delay. Unless a Rune of this type actually falls in the Result Position, however, TIR will generally carry the day.

For a female querent, this Rune often indicates the influence of a strong and determined man — who will either be a great support to her in her present trouble, or who will actively help her out of her difficulties. Sometimes, this man is her immediate superior, sometimes a colleague: always he is someone she respects or looks up to in some way. Since the most effective backing a woman can have is the support of someone she loves, TIR frequently represents a boyfriend, live-in lover, husband or father — depending, of course, on her age and status.

In a woman's runecast, when TIR is paired with LAGU (or sometimes — in a runecast like Asking the Norns where no pairing takes place — when these Runes fall next to each other), initiative moves to the querent and she is shown acting on her own behalf. In this situation, TIR upright signifies that she is prepared to fight for her rights; that she sees herself in a morally superior position, etc. — all the meanings, in fact, that are associated with TIR for a male querent.

Conversely, when reading for a man, TIR in association with MANN either by pairing or close proximity, can signify help from a superior or workmate, or from powerful friends.

As most people are aware, Mars also has a sexual connotation. In certain areas of botany and biology, the astrological symbol of Mars is used to identify male specimens, while the astrological symbol of Venus is used to identify female ones. Additionally, in graffiti and on badge designs these two symbols are used to denote sexual union or sexual affinity. Because of this close association with sexuality, TIR is a prime significator of physical attraction and sexual compatibility. Thus, TIR upright is an excellent omen for all questions relating to romance, since it indicates passion allied with fidelity, affection, and emotional happiness.

Because TIR is predominantly a masculine Rune, in any question relating to love or marriage it will represent the male half of the sexual equation, irrespective of the sex of the querent. Thus, if the querent is male, TIR will represent him, and if the querent is female, it will represent the man in her life.

Where there is more than one man in a female querent's life, TIR will represent the man she is most interested in — the one she feels most passionate about — *at the time of the reading*. This will usually be the one who has only lately come into her life — the lover rather than the husband; the new boyfriend rather than the old steady. Judge of this man's intentions by TIR's position — upright means honourable; reversed means dishonourable — and by looking at the Rune with which TIR is paired. In this way, you will be able to find out such things as whether the relationship is based *only* on sexual attraction (paired with PEORTH reversed), and whether it will lead to lasting happiness (paired with WYNN).

Since physical union is the source of procreation, TIR is also associated with fertility and increase. This can refer not only to the fertility of the body, but also to the fertility of the mind — and since TIR is a Victory-rune, it often indicates creative ideas constructively applied. For those with farming or agricultural interests, this Rune can also refer to the fertility of the earth, and the growth of crops.

Reversed

In reverse, TIR represents the lack, or negation, of those qualities it signifies when upright. It therefore stands for waning enthusiasm, failure in competitive enterprises, and lack of fidelity in matters of love and friendship.

As with the upright interpretation, TIR reversed will often shed much light on a male querent's state of mind. In this case, however, it reveals that the querent is inclined to quit in the face of difficulties. Nor is he much interested in making effort on his own behalf. On the contrary, he often expects rewards to drop into his lap by divine right — and if results are not immediately forthcoming in anything he undertakes, he gives up. It can have the same meaning for a female querent where TIR reversed is found paired or closely associated with LAGU.

When representing a state of mind, this Rune may sometimes fall reversed in a runecast surrounded by positive Runes. This generally signifies that the situation is going to turn out well despite the querent's present despondency and lack of optimism.

In reverse, TIR is a Rune indicative of impatience. Often, it counsels the querent not to give in, but to try a little harder for a little longer. When paired with Delay-runes, or hemmed in by them in an otherwise positive runecast, it usually indicates that the querent is experiencing 'the dark before the dawn'; and if the querent is patient the dawn will break.

In questions of love, TIR reversed signifies that any liaison in which the querent is presently involved in unlikely to reach a permanent conclusion. The reversal of this Rune is an indication of dwindling masculine passion for (as the medieval astrological texts point out) the negative action of Mars is fiery and passionate but soon over.

For married querents, TIR's reversal betokens the onset of a period of misunderstandings and difficulties in communication. Depending on the tone of the other Runes in the cast, this situation may result in either separation and divorce or eventual reconciliation.

Of course, these meanings only apply when the querent has specifically asked for guidance in romantic or matrimonial problems, or when TIR falls reversed in the Fifth or Seventh House of an Astrological runecast accompanied by other negative Runes. In other positions or related to other questions, the reversal of this Rune may point to setbacks and difficulties in some other area of life.

TIR reversed often signifies an impeded flow of energy on one level or another. On a physical level, it can indicate the need for an operation — though this need not necessarily have been recognized by either the querent or his doctor — or it may imply barrenness and sterility. Sometimes — though of course not always, it can indicate male infertility or impotence. On a psychological level, this Rune may signify that the querent is nervous or accident prone — and this is particularly so when OTHEL reversed is near at hand. And on a mental level, TIR reversed may represent barrenness of ideas, sterility of thought when it comes to creative projects — both of which are indicative of a stifled energy-flow.

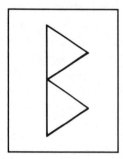

Alternatives	: ᛒ
Letter	: B
Name	: BEORC
Meaning	: A Birch Tree
Planetary Rulerships	: The Moon and Jupiter

As we saw when examining the correspondence of the Rune FEOH, the moon is a symbol of the Great Mother, the principle of fecundity in nature. It is not surprising, therefore, to discover that the keyword for BEORC is *generation*, both in the sense 'to give birth to' and used as a demarcation between one age group and another.

The birch was a tree of inception to the European races. For the Celts, the birch represented the first month of the new year, as Robert Graves points out in the relevant section of *The White Goddess*. BEORC is also a Rune of inception or birth, in contrast to LAGU, which (as we shall see) is a Rune of *conception*. BEORC is a fertility Rune, and always indicates a physical birth, either of a child or an idea. Naturally, it is a good omen for this Rune to fall upright in a runecast where the querent is expecting a child or is hopeful of conceiving. Otherwise, it suggests that any schemes the querent may have been mulling over should be implemented right away; or — in a Gate of Heaven runecast — in the month signified by BEORC's placement, for this Rune represents both parturition and the growth and development of an idea or undertaking. BEORC is always indicative of a *tangible* result. For a young couple, this may mean the birth of a child; for a farmer it could signify the growth of crops or an increase in live-stock.

BEORC is a Rune which governs both mother and child. In particular, it relates to that period in infancy when the mother is feeding and controlling her offspring, for this Rune is intimately connected with all matters to do with infants and the very young. Because of this, BEORC is said to have such meanings as: to nourish; to nurse; to feed; to tend, care for, or look after.

When not referring to the physical birth of a child, BEORC often indicates a project in the early stages of development — when it is still young and vulnerable and in need of constant attention like a child in infancy. Since it represents new growth, BEORC is a particularly helpful influence under which to initiate new schemes or enterprises.

Because the secondary ruler of BEORC is Jupiter, the Rune generally indicates a fortunate outcome to any question asked when it falls in the Result Position in a runecast. Sometimes, however, it will signify a scheme that needs to be nursed along if it is to succeed, and that success will not be automatic even though there will be no active opposition to it as such.

In other positions in a runecast, BEORC merely indicates a beginning, often a beginning that brings much happiness, or the beginning of a cherished project. Future progress, however, must be judged from associated Runes — particularly those following after BEORC. Negative Runes will indicate that the querent's project or undertaking will be short-lived; while positive Runes presage a successful conclusion.

In its other meaning of generation, which segregates particular age groups, BEORC can represent a member of the immediately preceding generation — either the father or the mother. However, since the Rune is so closely associated with the idea of birth, it generally signifies the querent's mother, emphasizing once again the link between mother and child. Also, BEORC may represent a member of the immediately *succeeding* generation, i.e. one of the querent's children. If your intuition gives you no clue as to which generation is intended, it is better to say that domestic or family matters will be important to the querent over the period designated.

Due to the influence of Jupiter, the secondary ruler of BEORC, this Rune usually indicates a fortunate happening within the family circle — often a family celebration of a birth, christening, engagement or wedding. Alternatively, BEORC can show something happening to the querent which will cause rejoicing among the immediate family. Depending on the accompanying Runes, this can be anything from a promotion to a win on the pools.

This Rune is often indicative of the home-maker. Thus it may describe the querent's own personality, but — especially for the male querent — it will often represent the wife or mother. Sometimes, BEORC can represent the querent's home — though it usually refers to the 'family' home. BEORC stands for the concept of home rather than an actual house, as reflected in the saying 'home is where the heart is'; so this description may sometimes lead to confusion. An unmarried querent living in a bed-sitter, for instance, may still think of their parent's house as 'home'. The same thing applies to the concept of family: mention the word 'family' to an unmarried querent and they will invariably think of their parents and siblings, etc; whereas a married querent with children of their own will tend to think of their own spouse and offspring.

Reversed

When reversed, BEORC is the harbinger of family problems and domestic troubles. It promotes friction and disputes between the querent and their nearest and dearest, but because the two planets ruling this Rune are by nature harmonious, the presence of BEORC reversed in a runecast does not, on its own, point to *permanent* splits or irreconcilable differences. In order for such an outcome to be indicated, BEORC would need to be surrounded by other negative Runes — or at least paired with an inauspicious Rune.

Usually, BEORC reversed forecasts an unfortunate event affecting the family, often a family gathering occasioned by illness or death. Sometimes it can signify the receipt of worrying news concerning a member of the family —

a parent or child, or (for a male querent) the wife.

Frequently, BEORC reversed will represent the querent's anxiety over the health or general well-being of a relative or child. Exactly who this person is can be judged either from the accompanying Runes (ANSUR for a child; GEOFU for the marriage partner, etc.), or in an Astrological runecast, from the House in which BEORC is situated (Fifth House for a child; Fourth House for the mother; Ninth House for the father; and Seventh House for the spouse).

If the Rune with which BEORC is paired is negative, or if other indications in the runecast are pessimistic, then you should advise the querent to have the health of the relative about whom they are concerned checked. Bear in mind, however, that BEORC reversed is a *warning* and not a portent of irrevocable doom. If the querent can get the said relative to their doctor as quickly as possible, it is likely that the ailment can be cleared up quite rapidly with the correct medication.

The same thing applies to questions relating to pregnancy. BEORC reversed may indicate sterility — usually on the part of the female partner — but it refers to *malfunction* rather than congenital infertility; and that malfunction can generally be rectified with medical aid — or, sometimes, minor surgery.

Where the querent or the querent's wife is already pregnant, BEORC reversed suggests a miscarriage or an abortion. However, forewarned is forearmed; and you should advise the woman in question to take special care of her health during the period of gestation — not to overexert herself in any way and to keep off her feet as much as possible. *DON'T* mention the possibility of miscarriage or you may aggravate the situation by disturbing someone who is already in a highly sensitized and suggestible state.

Because the upright Rune is associated with the growth and development of children, the appearance of BEORC reversed can indicate worry over some aspect of a child's welfare. As already stated, this can sometimes relate purely to health matters, but it may also signify worry about the child's mental, moral, or scholastic development.

Where a question relates solely to business, and BEORC appears reversed in a placement which obviously does not refer to the querent's domestic affairs, it generally indicates that any new business venture contemplated at the time of the reading will fall through. Either the querent's plans will be stillborn or they will never amount to anything substantial. Remember, however, that even in reverse BEORC is not an entirely unfortunate Rune; and if other factors in the runecast counsel prudence and restraint, such plans can sometimes be brought to fruition at some other time.

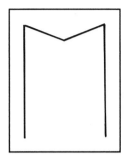

Alternatives : ⼂

Letter : Eo

Name : EOH

Meaning : A Horse

Planetary Rulership : Mercury (Active)

Astrologically speaking, Mercury is a planet of change, and the main significance of EOH is 'a change for the better'. Often it will indicate a planned change, one that the querent is already anticipating at the time of the reading. Indeed, when EOH is placed in a prominent position such as the First House in an Astrological runecast, it may be that the querent's main purpose in having a reading at all is to seek advice concerning a contemplated change.

What this change may be will differ from reading to reading, but since EOH means 'horse', the change generally involves travel in some shape or form. It may imply a change of home or a change of job, usually coupled with a change of location — borough, town, or even country.

It can also mean a journey, particularly by land. This, again, is related to EOH's meaning 'a horse'. The presence of other Journey-Runes, such as RAD and ANSUR, will indicate where this interpretation is to be preferred, as well as hinting at the reason for such a journey: RAD suggests a holiday; ANSUR reversed, a visit to a sick relative; BEORC, a family occasion — probably a christening or a wedding.

The appearance of EOH in a prominent place in a runecast often intimates that the querent is tackling their problem in the right spirit and advises them to continue in the same manner. It usually indicates that the querent is fast approaching their goal — that they are almost home and dry.

Sometimes, in association with a Rune signifying advice or outside help (such as ANSUR, JARA or MANN) it can show that the querent will be aided to success by another person whose good judgement and common sense can be relied upon.

Reversed
The implication of EOH reversed depends entirely on the sort of Runes with which it finds itself associated. It is the one Rune which does not automatically reverse its meaning when it falls upside down, and should it be grouped with positive Runes, it can have exactly the same signification as when upright.

Sometimes it denotes a far journey: a journey by sea (or in these days, by air). This is especially so when EOH is paired with LAGU — though if RAD is also in the picture, it may signify an extended holiday rather than emigration.

In some circumstances — such as when EOH reversed is paired with a Rune of sudden change, like UR — it may represent an unplanned or unanticipated change. However, this change need not be an unhappy or unhelpful one, unless there are also negative Runes in the runecast.

But when EOH falls reversed in a totally inauspicious runecast, it then implies an alteration for the worse. In such circumstances, you should counsel the querent not to implement any changes they may be contemplating, as these are likely to result only in misfortune and loss.

Divination Practice
The Four Quarters

This runecast gives a detailed look at a situation. It is especially good for complicated problems that spill over into several areas of life — such as a career move which involves uprooting the family.

Timing
Approximately six months into the past, and six months into the future. As always, however, much depends on the nature of the problem.

Delay-Runes in the Result Position show either that the situation will not be resolved within six months, or that it will not be resolved within what the querent thinks of as a reasonable time.

Method
Place the Runes on your diviner's cloth. Make sure they are all face down. Swirl, select eleven at random, and lay them out as shown in Figure 11. As you will see, despite its name this runecast is made up of four *parts* rather than four actual quarters.

Turn over the Central Rune (position 11). This will give you the essential 'tone' of the reading — or it may state quite baldly what the reading is to be about: what the querent has on their mind. If SIGEL appeared in this position, for example, the reading would most likely be concerned mainly with health matters.

Secondly, look at the Runes in positions 1, 2 and 10. These positions constitute the first 'quarter', and represent the querent, their abilities and characteristics, as well as their mental and emotional state at the time of the reading. You will need to synthesize the meanings of these three Runes in order to make a coherent assessment of this quarter. This is slightly more difficult than dealing with pairs of Runes, but your task will be made easier by the fact that the Rune in position 1 carries more weight than either of the other two Runes.

Thus, if the Rune in position 2 were positive, and the Rune in position 10 were negative, then the Rune in position 1 would tip the balance in one direction or the other depending on whether Rune 1 were itself positive or negative. Of course, if the Rune in position 1 turned out to be a non-reversible

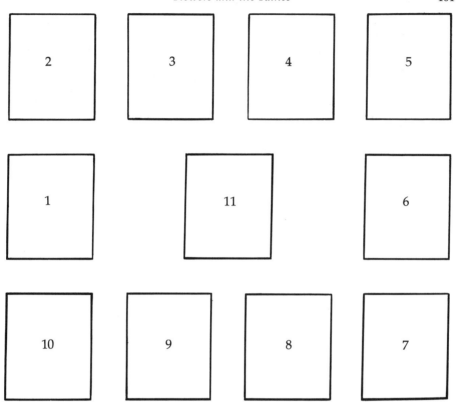

Figure 11: The Four Quarters

Rune, you would have to check to see if this Rune had anything in common with either of the other two, and make your assessment accordingly.

For instance, if GEOFU fell between UR and BEORC reversed, you might align GEOFU and BEORC because they both indicate 'married love' — and the indications would not be promising in that direction. If you were really adventurous, you might also associate UR, as representing a promotion or chance to get ahead, with GEOFU as 'business partnership', and read the whole grouping as: 'Great strides have been made in your business life, but this has caused you to neglect your family, which could lead to trouble unless you take steps to redress the balance forthwith.'

Sometimes, an uninspiring first quarter will show that the querent is in an undecided frame of mind as to how their future will develop; that they are only too aware of the risks involved in what they are doing. Do not, therefore, be at all surprised to find combinations of positive, negative and non-reversible Runes (or even all non-reversible Runes) in this quarter.

Next, turn to the Runes in positions 5, 6 and 7. These form the second quarter and represent either the opposition that the querent can expect to meet, or the thoughts and actions of other people most closely involved with the problem. Thus, in questions pertaining to romance, the first quarter will represent the querent and the second quarter will represent the loved one. Again, the three Runes which comprise the second quarter should be read as a group, with the middle Rune (position 6) carrying a marginally greater emphasis than the other two Runes.

If the indications of both the first and second quarters are negative (i.e. if they *individually* contain a majority of negative Runes), the outlook does not appear promising. If the first quarter is positive and the second quarter negative, the querent will meet formidable opposition, and you will need to judge which quarter is the stronger in order to determine the result. Where you are unable to do this, it is permissible to use the Central Rune (position 11) as arbitrator.

If the first quarter is negative and the second quarter positive, the querent doubts their own ability and is fearful of future developments. When the Rune in position 11 is fortunate, or where the second quarter is stronger than the first, circumstances will turn in the querent's favour and the matter conclude happily without the querent having to take much of an active role themselves. If both quarters are in the main positive, then the querent has nothing to worry about, since their efforts are bound to be crowned with success.

The first and second quarters usually show the situation to date, often with clear indications as to how matters came to reach their present condition.

Positions 3 and 4 form the third quarter and are read as a pair. This should give you few problems, as by now you ought to be used to pairing Runes. The third quarter indicates how the matter can be expected to continue. Depending on the type of question posed, you can think of this quarter as symbolizing the near future — 'What happens next'.

Runes 8 and 9 are also read as a pair. This is the fourth quarter and represents the far future, or Result. This is the first time you have had to pair Runes in a Result Position, and it may give you a few problems in interpretation to begin with. Simply remember that such a thing as partial success is possible. The Runes will indicate in what area the querent's hopes will be fulfilled, and in what area they will be disappointed.

Non-reversible Runes falling in the fourth quarter should be read as for their appearance in a Result Position as outlined in their appropriate sections in the text. GEOFU falling here, for instance, is generally a good sign even if the query does not relate to love or partnerships of any kind, for it can indicate the kind of inner and outer harmony that we all experience when things are going our way.

Chapter 7

NUMEROLOGY AND THE RUNES

All the Runes of the Elder Futhark are attributed to one of the single numbers 1 to 9, the only exception being the Blank Rune which was not originally a member of the runic alphabet. Since there are twenty-five Runes and only nine digits, it is obvious some Runes must share the same number. In runic numerology the numbers 1 to 7 are allocated according to the days of the week starting on Sunday, so that the number 1 is equivalent to the Sun (Sun day), the number 2 to the Moon (Moon day), 3 to Mars or Tiw (Tiw's day), 4 to Mercury or Odin (Woden's day), 5 to Jupiter or Thor (Thor's day), 6 to Venus or Freyja (Freyja's day) and 7 to Saturn or the Norns. Saturday is the only day to receive a Latin name. The numerals 8 and 9, which fall outside the seven day week system are allotted to Skoll and Hati, the wolves who constantly pursue the Sun and Moon across the Heavens seeking to devour them and thus bring about the end of the present age.

This method of allocation provides a fairly simple method for remembering the number ascribed to each Rune, since generally speaking the number allotted is that of the prime planetary influence ascribed to the Rune. In those cases where a Rune has two planets sharing rulership, the prime influence is the planet mentioned *first* in the text.

Thus, SIGEL and DAEG correspond to the number 1, and BEORC and LAGU to the number 2. The Runes UR, KEN, PEORTH and TIR are ruled by 3, while 4 has dominion over ANSUR, RAD, JARA and EOH. THORN and YR vibrate to the number 5, while 6 is the number associated with the Venus Runes, FEOH, GEOFU, WYNN and ING. The number 7 is that of NIED and OTHEL, 8 is allocated to HAGALL and MANN, while 9 is ascribed the Runes IS and EOLH. The Blank Rune indicates an unknown period of time, usually one well outside the timespan of the current reading.

These numbers are used in a runecast to give the diviner some idea of when a predicted event is likely to come about. Let us imagine that we are using the runecast Mimir's Head, which reads three months into the future. If the Rune FEOH appears upright in the Result Position, this would indicate that a successful outcome could be expected to any query concerning either love or money within six days or six weeks, because the number associated with FEOH is 6. I should warn you, however, that the time factor is not always to be found so easily, and you will still have to rely on your intuition to tell you whether six days or six weeks or, in runecasts with a longer time span, six months or six years is intended.

This is only one facet of an absorbing subject which really deserves a book to itself. I have outlined the above system because it is the one I have found to be most reliable for timing in runic divination. Those students who would like to know more about this branch of runic lore, especially that aspect of it relating to runic magic, in which the Runes are allotted the numbers 1 to 24 consecutively, are referred to Edred Thorsson's *Futhark: A Handbook of Runic Magic*, details of which can be found in the Bibliography.

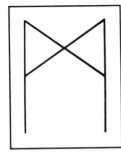

Alternatives   : ᛈᛘ ᛏ ᛦ
Letter   : M
Name   : MANN
Meaning   : Mankind
Planetary Rulerships : Saturn and the
                      South Node

The literal translation of Mann is *mankind*, and the Teutonic shaman meant by this to imply the interdependence of the race; for they believed that no individual could ever be entirely self-sufficient. They perceived life to be not chaos, but a pattern — a pattern in which each member of society had their part to play, and where the smooth running of affairs, both public and private, was dependent upon each person finding their allotted role and fulfilling it to the best of their ability.

Since MANN is a Rune of interdependence, it will often indicate that the querent can expect to receive the assistance or co-operation of a fellow human being which will be of considerable aid to them in the resolution of their difficulties. According to the Teutonic astrologers, Saturn and the South Node share certain characteristics. Both are cold, aloof, impersonal and objective, and due to these influences, the Rune MANN generally signifies impersonal advice, objective aid, or (sometimes) altruistic assistance. When this rune appears upright in a reading, you may be sure that there is no ulterior motive behind the help offered, and that any advice tendered to the querent will be honest and reliable.

Saturn also represents duty; and for this reason MANN regularly turns up in a runecast to indicate a person who gives help as part of their job. Thus, it may signify a doctor, accountant, bank manager, or lawyer; and can, in fact, represent any form of paid-help right down to the child-minder or daily help who frees the querent to do other things.

But MANN does not always indicate another person. Since the querent is by definition a member of the human race, this Rune can sometimes relate to qualities within the enquirer themselves. Sometimes, MANN intimates that the querent needs to look more dispassionately at their present predicament; that they are becoming too deeply involved, and are allowing the situation to get out of proportion. In conjunction with negative Runes, it may signify that the problem is threatening to swamp the querent. One of the best ways to get things back into perspective, of course, is to seek an outside opinion — which is what this Rune suggests should be done.

MANN has strong connections with the power of thought, for it is mankind's ability to think and to reason which marks us off from all the other species on this planet. In fact, the generic classification of mankind is *homo sapiens* — Thinking Man. The two main differences in the way mankind thinks in comparison with other animals are: the power to think logically (which is ruled by Saturn), and the power to think creatively (which is ruled by the South Node). It is for this reason that MANN indicates that the querent needs to bring logic to bear on their problem, and to look at their situation more dispassionately.

From the point of view of creative thought, MANN often suggests that there is much that the querent can do to improve or alleviate the circumstances in which they find themselves by the adoption of a more positive and forward-looking attitude — even when there appears to be nothing that can be done on the physical plane.

The correct use of the powers of creative visualization is one of the great secrets of magical training, and represents the ability to influence events by non-physical means. Thus, MANN is indicative of magical power or potential — particularly when it falls in the First House of a Life Reading — just as PEORTH will signify mediumistic talent and LAGU clairvoyant ability in the same circumstances.

Being a Rune of interdependence, it is not surprising to find that MANN is concerned with equality in all its forms. For instance, when falling in the First House of an Astrological runecast, it will normally indicate that the querent is an avid supporter of human rights and civil liberties; and that they have a deep and (in the main) selfless concern for the well-being of all mankind.

As we saw when examining the Rune NIED, the planet Saturn is firmly linked to the concept of time. Because of this, MANN sometimes indicates that the querent's plans should be executed or their ideas put into action 'at the right time'. Other runes in the cast will give you a clue as to when that 'right time' may be. With positive Runes, MANN can indicate that the time for action is *now*; but with negative Runes — particularly Delay-Runes such as THORN, ANSUR reversed, NIED, ICE, BEORC reversed or OTHEL reversed — it signifies that the querent should postpone taking any action or making any important decisions for eight days, eight weeks or eight months, according to the nature of the question posed.

Reversed
MANN reversed indicates that the querent can expect no assistance from his or her fellow human beings over the period covered by the reading or, in the case of the Gate of Heaven runecast, during the month indicated by the position of the Rune. On the contrary, the querent is likely to meet with obstructionism, the subversion of their aims and the sabotage of their plans. Sometimes, the querent is the victim of a group of people, but it is more usual to find that these activities emanate from a single individual, whom the querent will inevitably regard as an enemy.

The Rune paired with MANN or immediately following it will suggest the best way to counteract this influence. Thus, paired with THORN or NIED, the advice would be to keep a low profile, to play a waiting game and watch for future developments; but paired with JARA the advice would be to invoke the law; and with TIR to fight fire with fire.

Because MANN shows the querent possessing or sharing the qualities of which it is indicative, this Rune's message when in reverse can be that the querent is their own worst enemy. This may be due to excessive pessimism, lack of self-confidence, lack of faith in the future, or good old fashioned pig-headedness in some direction. When relating directly to the querent (by such means as appearing in the First House of an Astrological runecast, or in a position signifying the querent's attitude to the current situation), MANN reversed is a prime significator of selfishness. Generally, this selfishness is a symptom of the desire to cut oneself off from the rest of humanity — the 'Ivory Tower' syndrome. This is a negative manifestation of the powers of objectivity, dispassionate assessment and impersonal involvement denoted by the upright Rune, and it is often triggered initially by a reaction against man's inhumanity to man. To the Teutonic mind, however, this was a retrograde step; for they believed that the way forward for humanity lay through co-operation, not isolation.

MANN is a Rune which serves to remind us of the essential humanity — and therefore equality — of *every member* of the race and, occasionally, in readings concerning personal relationships, the message of MANN reversed is, 'You are taking the wrong attitude. Try seeing things from the other person's point of view.'

The injunction that the querent should carry out plans at the right time is even more imperative when MANN is upside down — and again a delay of eight days, eight weeks or eight months is generally advisable.

Like the North Node, the South Node represents all things that are alien to the querent, and for that reason MANN reversed can signify a foreign country or a foreigner or a person whose whole way of life is totally alien to that of the querent. This individual is not necessarily evil — just different. Indeed, since 'opposites attract', the person represented by this Rune often holds a certain fascination for the querent — and where the two are of opposite sexes there is inevitably a degree of romantic interest. In an otherwise propitious runecast, this is often the meaning of MANN reversed.

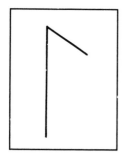

Alternatives	: ⱶ
Letter	: L
Name	: LAGU
Meaning	: Water
Planetary Rulership	: The Moon

When occult philosophers divide existence into the four conditions of Earth, Air, Water and Fire, commonly called the Four Elements, the Element of Water represents the liquid or fluidic state. By analogy, all things that equate with that state are also under the dominion of Elemental Water. Occult philosophy sees Water as a feminine (that is to say, a passive or receptive) Element, and in addition, most people are aware of the connection which exists between the Moon and menstruation, the cycle of generation in women. These two facts do much to explain the associations and attributions of LAGU, for this Rune corresponds to the amniotic fluid and, as such, often acts as a significator of conception as well as being precursor to the birth which is to follow it.

Symbolically both the Moon and Elemental Water represent the subconscious aspect of the mind, that part of the psyche from whence intuition and the psychic powers in general arise. For this reason the appearance of LAGU in a prominent position in a cast often signifies that the querent should be willing to follow their intuition in the matter under review. Falling in the First House of an Astrological runecast, it frequently indicates that the querent has very definite psychic abilities (for the duration of the period covered by the reading at any rate), and that he or she is under the guidance or direction of the Higher Powers, their Spirit Guides, Inner Plane Contacts, or whatever nomenclature you are accustomed to using. Sometimes the querent will be made directly aware of this guidance, though this is not always the case. Where the querent is naturally psychic or has latent psychic abilities, however, it is not unusual for them to receive such guidance directly through clairvoyance, clairaudience, psychometry, etc. While, for those who are not naturally psychic, this Rune often presages a significant dream or premonition concerning a potentially dangerous situation or offer.

In circumstances where the querent possesses no psychic awareness whatsoever (and many men are unwilling to admit that they ever function on this level), LAGU will generally indicate success in some area of activity which employs the imaginative faculty. This may be in the sphere of art, design, music or the writing of fiction, anything which draws its creative impetus from the depths of the subconscious. Also, since Water is classified as a plastic Element (because liquids accommodate themselves to the shape of the container in which they are stored), LAGU can indicate success through acting, since an actor, too, has to mould himself to the role he is asked to play.

Because Water is a receptive Element, LAGU in a Result Position often signifies that the querent will meet with a sympathetic and understanding response from other people involved in their problem which will hasten the situation to a successful conclusion.

The receptivity of Water is also responsible for the fact that this Rune often depicts an ability to absorb and retain. A prominent LAGU is the sign of a good memory and is thus most useful for all matters connected with learning and education. It is an excellent omen for any querent with academic aspirations, especially when it is found in association with ANSUR. But LAGU indicates not only a person who receives teaching (as in psychic guidance) or who has the ability to take in and store information, it also indicates the type of person who is able to pass on information coherently and effectively. Thus, it is sometimes called 'the Teacher's Rune'.

Since Water represents fluidity, LAGU frequently indicates that the querent should not be afraid to 'go with the flow'. For, as the poet puts it, 'There is a tide in the affairs of men which, taken at the flood, leads on to fortune,' and therefore, the appearance of LAGU in a prominent position in a runecast generally signifies that the tide has turned in the enquirer's favour.

Just as TIR is the prime masculine significator, so is LAGU the prime feminine significator. Often it will symbolize the female querent herself, while for a male querent it can denote the most important woman in his life — mother, sweetheart, wife or even, on occasion, a daughter.

For a female querent, LAGU upright indicates that, no matter what problems beset her at the time of the reading, she is more than capable of facing up to them. For, when LAGU falls upright in a woman's runecast it signifies that she has no doubt at all as to her own ability to cope practically and efficiently with any contingencies which may arise.

When reading for a man, LAGU upright often hints at the presence in the background of a supportive female, one who is at once loving and wise, sympathetic and practical.

Reversed
Unless backed up by strongly positive Runes, LAGU reversed is an unlucky omen. It often indicates that the querent has been misled by their intuitions or inner feelings into branching out into some area of life for which they have no real aptitude. By attempting to develop talents they do not in fact possess, or possess only to a minimal degree, the querent is most probably overstraining both their physical reserves and their material resources. You may have some difficulty, however, in persuading them that this is so, especially in those situations revolving around either a love affair or the development of their own psychic faculties. In these two cases particularly, the enquirer will usually be convinced that the exact opposite is true.

Unless the runecast also contains Runes counselling delay, LAGU reversed warns that it would be disastrous for the querent to adopt a 'wait and see' attitude to events. Immediate action should be implemented by the querent with a view to extricating themselves from any situation in which they may have become entangled. For, in reverse, LAGU is a Rune of temptation — temptation to do the wrong things, to take the easy way out, to evade one's responsibilities. However, it also signifies that, should the querent yield to any of these temptations, the matter will not go undetected. Eventually the miscreant will be required to pay a heavy price for their indiscretion or misdemeanour, and if JARA is also close at hand, the discovery will be made all the sooner. The appearance of LAGU reversed is often an indication that the querent would prefer to take the line of least resistance without being fully aware that this course of action will lead only to unhappiness, failure and loss of self-respect.

For a female querent, LAGU reversed is frequently indicative of a timerous and fearful nature. In association with other negative Runes, LAGU reversed suggests that the woman in question is given to lurid imaginings which further exacerbate her tendency to vacillation and fearfulness. Occasionally (when falling in the Seventh or Eleventh House of an Astrological runecast, for instance), LAGU reversed may refer not to the querent herself but to a female friend or associate. It will then warn of enmity from this woman, duplicity and betrayal on the part of an erstwhile female friend.

For the male enquirer also, this Rune can act as a warning of treachery from a woman. In a man's runecast, LAGU reversed regularly heralds the appearance in the querent's life of a temptress, a siren who will lure him to disaster. Sometimes, however, in an otherwise positive runecast, especially when surrounded by Success-Runes, it can indicate a managing woman who helps the querent to achieve his goal, but to whom he will be made to feel beholden and inferior for ever after.

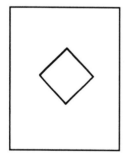

Alternatives	: □ ○ ◇ ⋈
Letter	: Ng
Name	: ING
Meaning	: The God Ing
Planetary Rulership	: Venus (Passive)

I prefer to use the older symbol for this Rune rather than the Anglo-Saxon variant because, to my mind, a totally enclosed glyph nicely sums up the essential meaning of ING, which is *completion*. It is a Rune which indicates the successful conclusion of a plan or enterprise. But it also represents the sense of relief which accompanies the completion of any task and, by extension, may indicate a mind set free from worries or anxiety without necessarily referring to a state of completion at all.

ING is another of those Runes that do not have a reversed meaning, and there are many types of completion — fortunate and unfortunate. However, ING is an almost wholly fortuitous Rune, and only in an extremely negative runecast does it imply that the querent's efforts will end in failure.

Ing was a god of fertility, and the runic symbol itself represents the scrotum, the male seed-bag. For this reason ING is also a Fertility-rune and — depending on the associated Runes — can signify the birth of a child, a new job or love affair, or the commencement of a fresh stage in the querent's life.

At first glance, this Rune appears to signify two contradictory events — termination and birth. However, ING invariably indicates the ending of one phase of activity so that a new, and happier, one can begin. It is a highly significant Rune, especially in the smaller runecasts, for it can signal the arrival of an event which will prove to be an important milestone in the querent's life.

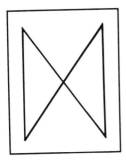

Alternatives	: ᚻ ᛞ
Letter	: D
Name	: DAEG
Meaning	: Day
Planetary Rulership	: The Sun and the North Node

The heat of the Sun in spring and summer is responsible for the growth of vegetation, and DAEG, too, is symbolic of increase and growth. Depending on the position in which DAEG falls and the type of Runes with which it is associated, this growth may occur in any area of the querent's life. It may be connected with a relationship, an investment, or an aspect of their career; but, generally, it is a fortunate development, and one which the querent willingly accepts and approves of wholeheartedly.

Unlike the Moon, whose waxing and waning can be followed nightly, changes in the Sun's strength are far less perceptible on a day-to-day basis. For this reason, the growth which DAEG betokens is often a slow and measured progress rather than an overnight success. On the other hand, the contrast between the seasons — especially in the northern climates inhabited by the Teutonic tribes — is as total as one could wish. Therefore, the difference between the situation foreshadowed by DAEG and the state of the querent's life at the time of the reading will often be as complete and heartening as the turning of winter into summer.

DAEG is a Rune which has much to do with *attitude*, and often it forecasts a change of mind or a change of heart on the querent's part. Since the Sun represents the ego in astrology, the change denoted is generally a self-activated one. Usually, this Rune will represent the querent resolving to make a new start on some level, though sometimes it will show that the querent has decided to accept and make the best of a situation over which they have no material control. In this latter case, so long as the right attitude is adopted, the querent's circumstances will gradually change for the better through the intervention of some outside agency.

In common with KEN and SIGEL, the two other runes having solar associations, DAEG suggests that the querent should project a sunny disposition in order to help them through their present difficulties. It signifies that a positive attitude will enable the querent to meet success half way. When a negative Saturn-ruled Rune is near at hand (WYNN reversed, HAGALL, MANN reversed or OTHEL reversed), DAEG indicates that the querent is thinking in terms of failure and obstacles to success, and is drawing these things to them in consequence.

The North Node also represents all those aspects of personality which have hitherto remained unexplored — either through wilful repression or ignorance of their existence. DAEG can show the querent being exposed to a different way of looking at the world, or to a novel and exciting philosophy of life (which may be religious or psychological, or the simple homespun variety). The North Node is the symbol of eclipse, and the Sun is the symbol of light. DAEG, therefore, bears the connotation of 'light after darkness', which may take the form of an intellectual enlightenment or of 'seeing the Light' in a religious sense.

This Rune has no negative aspect and its appearance in an otherwise depressing runecast often hints that the querent can still salvage something from the situation if they are willing to look within themselves. Though, sometimes, it can intimate that the querent should bow out of a situation while his pride is still intact, or while he still retains his physical and mental health. Whenever DAEG is associated or paired with Delay-Runes, however, it considerably alleviates their evil influence, since it points to eventual victory over obstacles and hindrances.

DAEG, as a symbol of growth, will often signify an increase of whatever is indicated by the Rune with which it is paired. For example: paired with ANSUR — an increase of knowledge; paired with BEORC — an addition to the family; with FEOH — an increase in wealth; with OTHEL — an increase in prestige.

When paired with reversed Runes, DAEG is not quite so easy to pin down. Occasionally, it will denote an increase in the querent's intransigence and perversity (particularly when paired with NIED or THORN reversed); but this is not always the case. Frequently, DAEG paired with a reversed Rune will simply imply that the good things promised by the upright meaning of the paired Rune *will* come about at some time, but not immediately. To put it another way: DAEG has the power to convert reversed Runes into Delay-Runes.

As is often the case with non-reversible Runes, you will have to rely on your intuition in the interpretation of DAEG. If your intuition won't work — or if it needs a helping hand — look to the following Runes in the cast for a clue: particularly the one holding the Result Position.

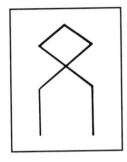

Alternatives :
Letter : O
Name : OTHEL
Meaning : A Possession
Planetary Rulerships : Saturn and Mars

OTHEL is the last Rune in the series, and in many ways it is the antithesis of the first runic symbol FEOH. Where FEOH represents money, OTHEL represents the things that money can buy.

The planet having primary rulership over this Rune is Saturn, the planet of limitation, and often the possessions symbolized by OTHEL have some limiting factor attached to them — such as being too large to be readily moved about. Thus the possession indicated by OTHEL is frequently either land or a building, or a part of a building: a house, maisonette, flat, warehouse, office space or business premises. Since the major item of property that most people get to possess is their own home, this Rune often indicates the querent's dwelling place — though sometimes it can indicate the family home, i.e. the house in which the querent was brought up.

Even when OTHEL does represent money — by falling in the Second House in an Astrological runecast, for instance — it indicates trusts, pension funds, long-term investments, or money tied up so that only a portion of it is available to the querent at the time of the reading. This may or may not please the querent, depending on the level of his immediate need for ready cash.

Saturn is a planet that has much to do with physical death. Thus, OTHEL can also indicate matters associated with death. It may represent a will, a legacy, or an heirloom — or some inherited possession not necessarily passing to the querent via a will. It may indicate something that has been in the family for generations, or which belonged to a parent or grandparent and which has been made over to the querent by Deed of Covenant or just simply given to them.

Usually the legacy betokened by OTHEL takes the form of property although this is not necessarily real estate rather than money — especially when either FEOH or PEORTH are near at hand. However, OTHEL can also stand for inherited psychological traits or physical characteristics, and the Rune paired with OTHEL will indicate what those traits are likely to be, and depending on

114

whether the Rune is upright or reversed, if they are a help or a hindrance to the querent.

Of the two planets ruling OTHEL, Saturn is persevering and Mars is energetic. Taken together, they symbolize *persistent effort*. Sometimes OTHEL indicates that the querent is a hard worker — as when found in the First House of an Astrological runecast, or when paired with SIGIL. Indeed if OTHEL is found in association with SIGEL, the querent may be a workaholic; but in any case this combination signifies a person who enjoys or is engrossed in their work; one who loves work and/or the material rewards it brings more than almost anything else in life. It is more usual, however, to find that OTHEL predicts that the querent will be expected to work hard in order to get what he wants out of life and to be where he wants to be.

When surrounded by materially oriented Runes like FEOH, WYNN, BEORC or NIED, this Rune is the sign of the miser or the materialist. Often, it represents a materialistic individual, one who is possessed by possessions — which is the other meaning of the word 'possession'. It shows a person caught in the trap of the consumer society and — oblivious of their predicament — willingly endeavouring to 'keep up with the Jones's'.

In association with intellectual Runes (ANSUR, MANN, and to a lesser extent RAD), OTHEL suggests that the querent is possessed by an ideal or vision. It generally depicts one who is single-minded in the pursuit of a goal — which may or may not be a good thing. A single-minded person is more likely to be a success in the world of commerce than someone who dissipates their energy; but a person who is fanatical on a single subject can just as easily be a crackpot or a psychopath as a captain of industry. The type of Rune paired with OTHEL, whether upright or reversed, will indicate which interpretation is most pertinent.

Upright, OTHEL promises the querent help from some Saturn-ruled quarter. Thus, it may signify assistance from older people — often an older relative — assistance from old-established firms or organizations, old established families, or old friends. Saturn also rules the establishment, the class system, vested interests and the Government — both the elected Government and the civil service — and so, under certain circumstances, help may come to the querent from one of those sources. OTHEL in the Sixth House of an Astrological runecast, for instance, often predicts the offer of a job in the civil service or local government, since the Sixth House is concerned with career.

Reversed
The main significance of OTHEL reversed is delay and frustration. With other negative Runes — especially those ruled by Saturn — OTHEL reversed may imply failure. On the other hand, in association with positive Runes, it merely indicates that success is further off than the querent anticipates. In such a case, the querent is generally well advised to sit matters out. Sometimes OTHEL reversed will indicate that more haste and less speed is what is required; that

the querent is tempted to cut corners when (in this particular instance) success depends on thoroughness and attention to detail.

OTHEL reversed in a prominent position in a runecast intimates that any attempt to progress too rapidly will only result in some accident or mishap which could either damage the querent's reputation or seriously curtail their chances of success.

Since progress through life can be compared with progress from one place to another, OTHEL reversed can also be taken as an indication of difficulties with travel, of inconveniences or the possibility of being involved in an accident. The placement of this Rune reversed in the Sixth, Eighth or Twelfth House of an Astrological runecast will often have this meaning, and the severity of the accident can be judged from the nature of the other Runes in the cast as well as from the House position of OTHEL itself — OTHEL in the Sixth House, for instance, not being as serious a portent as OTHEL in the Eighth. When found in the First or Third House of an Astrological runecast (or sometimes in their opposite Houses, the Seventh and Ninth) these accidents are often the fault of the querent's own inattention. It signifies jay-walking, impatience and recklessness.

In reverse, OTHEL is a Rune indicative of a person being forced to stand alone. It implies that the time has come when the querent is required to stand on their own two feet. In reverse, OTHEL can indicate that the querent has a 'Poor little rich girl (or boy)' attitude to life; for it sometimes signifies that the querent is at present involved in — or is about to run up against — a problem which they cannot buy their way out of. Alternatively, it can mean that the problem is one that cannot be overcome or got round by an appeal to one's parents, family, friends (the 'old boy' network, for instance), or the establishment. Often, in this latter case, OTHEL reversed indicates that recourse to law will be of no use to the querent no matter how strongly they believe themselves to be in the right, for, in reverse, this Rune indicates that one cannot buck the system, or use it to one's own advantage.

Divination Practice
Heimdale's Eight

This is a good runecast to use where you know absolutely nothing about a querent's background and circumstances. It is also helpful in questions where a somewhat complicated resolution of affairs is anticipated. This is because, having a four-Rune Result, Heimdale's Eight can give an extremely detailed description of the final outcome. It is also useful for assessing the strengths and weaknesses of the forces that oppose the querent, especially where weather conditions need to be taken into account — as in farming, gardening, holiday or travel questions.

Timing
Nine months into the future.

Method
Spread the Runes out face downwards on your diviner's cloth. Swirl, select sixteen, and lay them out as in Figure 12.

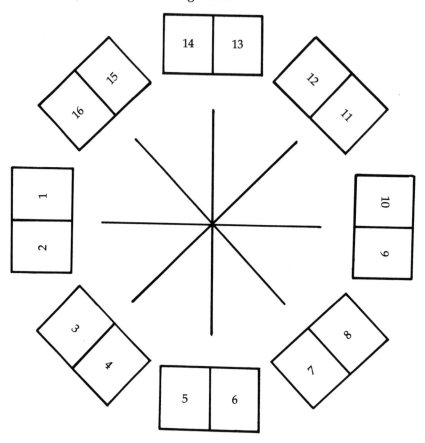

Figure 12: Heimdale's Eight

The first two Runes describe the querent's abilities and show what, if anything, they can do to advance or resolve the matter for themselves.

The second pair of Runes deal with the querent's psychology, their mental and/or emotional attitude to the situation.

The next two Runes given an insight into the causes behind the problem — or they may relate to events in the immediate past, usually within the preceding six months, though (as always) much depends on the nature of the problem.

Runes 7 and 8 indicate what opposition the querent can expect from outside circumstances, while Runes 9 and 10 show what opposition can be expected from other people. Positive Runes in either of these areas signify that there will be no opposition from that particular source. On the contrary, the querent can expect help and encouragement from those quarters.

Runes 15 and 16 represent the present, and are often indicative of the nature, or root, of the problem.

Runes 11 and 12 stand for the future, and Runes 13 and 14 indicate the Result. All four of these Runes should be carefully synthesized in order to reach a conclusion as to the outcome.

In circumstances where the needs of several people have to be considered, it is possible to designate a pair of Runes to represent each individual before you commence the reading. Thus Runes 1 and 2 would naturally be allotted to the querent, with Runes 9 and 10 representing the spouse or business partner, and Runes 7 and 8 signifying the querent's children, employees, or dependents, and so on.

Chapter 8

THE ANGLO-SAXON FUTHORK

Figure 13 shows the extended Futhark of thirty-three letters, sometimes called the Anglo-Saxon or Frisian Futhork. It is called a Futhork because, due to changes in dialect, the sound of ANSUR altered from a short A to a short O in the Anglo-Saxon language, and the symbol was renamed OS. The shape of the character was also amended slightly, as were several of the other Runes, i.e. KEN, HAGALL, JARA, SIGEL, ING and DAEG. The divinatory meanings of these symbols, however, remain the same.

If you have purchased a runeset based on the Anglo-Saxon designs you will still have only twenty-five runes, twenty-four Alphabet Runes plus one Blank Rune. You will be missing ING, and in its place you will have the twenty-fifth Rune of the Anglo-Saxon Futhork which is called AC (long A as in park). You may also have Rune thirty-one, an alternative K, in place of KEN. This character is exactly like a reversed EOLH, and for this reason both symbols (in this kind of runeset) are usually marked at the bottom with a nick to enable the reader to distinguish between them.

In theory it should be possible to make runecasts using all thirty-three Alphabet Runes but in practice it is usual to employ only twenty-four of them at any one time, either the twenty-four Runes of the Elder Futhark or the first twenty-five Runes of the Anglo-Saxon Futhork minus ING, plus the Blank Rune. The reason for this is tied up with Teutonic numerology and symbology. In a computer-orientated age we might say that twenty-four was the *modular number* of the Teutonic and Germanic peoples. That is to say that after twenty-four the potencies begin to repeat themselves. This can be deduced from the symbols themselves in many cases: letter twenty-six is the original symbol for ANSUR; letter twenty-seven is an UR with a small vertical dash inserted between its 'feet'; letter twenty-eight is one of the ancient alternatives for HAGALL; while, as we have already seen, letter thirty-one is a variant of KEN. Much the same applies to the remaining extra Runes; the duplication is not so obvious through an examination of their symbols but will become apparent when we come to look more closely at their magical/divinatory meanings.

Discover Runes

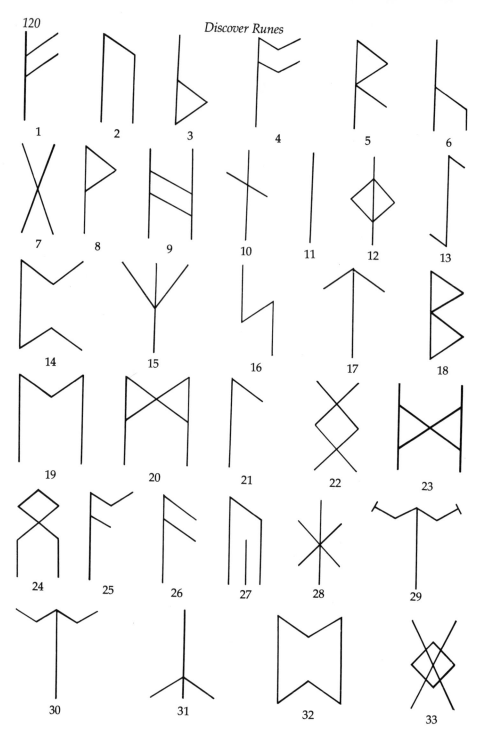

Figure 13: The Anglo-Saxon Futhork

These additional Runes have their uses but, like the majority of that great body of Symbol Runes from which the Alphabet Runes were originally selected, they are more suited to certain specialist forms of magic than to divination.

For those students in possession of an Anglo-Saxon runeset, I will describe the Rune AC in its divinatory meaning, and then make a few remarks about the other letters of the extended Futhork, mainly for the sake of completeness. But I want to make it clear that I do not advise the use of more than twenty-four Runes plus the Blank Rune — either the Elder Futhark itself or the amended twenty-four Runes of the Anglo-Saxon Futhork — for divination. Either you should use the set which includes ING or the set which includes AC, but do not try a combination of the two, and do not add further Runes from the Anglo-Saxon list. In my experience, such a procedure tends to a loss of clarity and accuracy in divination. So be warned and stick to the traditional methods.

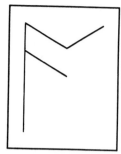

Alternatives	: —
Letter	: long A
Name	: AC
Meaning	: An Oak Tree
Planetary Rulership	: Mars in Scorpio

As can be seen, this planetary affinity is of a different order from those of the Elder Futhark. I think that the runemasters of Britain were hinting at a knowledge of the energies of Pluto. By which I do not mean that they knew of the existence of the planet bearing that name, but that they had had experience of the Plutonic forces. (This experience would be common to all Teutonic and Germanic shaman, but only the Anglo-Saxons seem to have 'gone public' with the knowledge.) Mars is the ruler of Scorpio in the Ptolemaic system, while Pluto assumes this position in modern astrological practice. Mars (Fire) in Scorpio (Water) is likely to produce a cloud of obscuring steam reminiscent of Pluto's helmet of invisibility in Greek mythology.

In a runecast, AC means the successful bypassing or negotiation of troubles. It does not suggest that the querent will make straight for their goal without experiencing a single hindrance or problem. There will be difficulties but they must be met with an attitude of compromise and a willingness to persuade others of the rightness of one's point of view, suitability or worthiness for a particular role, or whatever it is that one desires to do.

Mars is a fighter but in Scorpio it is not advisable for him to meet opposition head on. Either the querent must bring other people round to his way of thinking or, where possible, the enquirer must carry on 'doing their own thing' and prove themselves *by results*. When upright, this Rune intimates that, though problems exist, if the querent has the courage and strength of will to walk up to them, these problems will never fully materialize since the enquirer, metaphorically speaking, will be wearing the Helmet of Invisibility and can thus pass by unnoticed.

AC signifies success after difficulties so do not be surprised to discover reversed Runes preceding it in a cast. Reversed Runes coming after AC suggest that the querent does not possess sufficient courage to out-face their problems and, unless the reader is very persuasive indeed, will not attempt to do so, thus losing out. Sometimes this pattern of Runes indicates that the querent is not able to control their aggression, that they are either unable to compromise or unable to talk out their differences with others.

Those finding this Rune upright in a prominent position in their runecast should take as their watchword the martian motto, 'He who dares wins'.

Reversed

In reverse AC is an unpleasant symbol. It denotes a marked lack of success or progress of any kind, and often signifies the opposition of one's superiors or those in authority. It also shows that the querent has a problem with authority in general, being unable to accept it in any form. There is usually a pig-headed sort of independence which insists on doing things in its own way, rejecting all counsel and advice as 'interference'.

The best that can be done when AC reversed holds a prominent position in a runecast, is to play a waiting game and hope for conditions to turn in the querent's favour. Although the number associated with this Rune is 8, matters often begin to move again within three days, three weeks or three months; so AC must have some connection with the Norns, as well as with the secrets of runic proportions since these are eight units by three.

Letter:	short A
Name:	AESC
Meaning:	An Ash Tree

In Norse mythology the first human beings were created from an ash and an elm by the god Odin functioning in triad. Thus, this Rune emphasizes mankind's dependence on the gods, and is a restatement of ANSUR's message of tutelage, more oriented towards apprenticeship with a divine master than an earthly one.

Ygdrassil, the World Tree, was an ash, and the mysteries of this Rune are connected with free passage through all the Nine Worlds of the Teutonic cosmology either through astral projection or via the method known as Pathworking.

Letter:	Y
Name:	$\overline{YR}$
Meaning:	A Body Ornament

$\overline{YR}$ represents a brooch, a ring, a torque, a cuirass or a helmet — any type of body ornament that can be embellished with jewels or engraved with the signs or scenes intended to invoke victory. Like UR, it is concerned with summoning up the strength and will-power to do one's duty, to carry out a task laid upon one by others or by Fate.

Letter:	IO
Name:	IOR
Meaning:	Sea-Serpent

Jormungard was a huge serpent who lived in the deepest part of the ocean and was Thor's implacable enemy. In Norse mythology, even the giants were afraid of this awesome monster. Thus, IOR represents those things which are better left undisturbed by the magician unless he or she possesses the strength of Thor which will enable them to deal successfully with the consequences.

Letter:	EA
Name:	EAR
Meaning:	Ocean

This Rune personifies the destructive aspect of water. It is cold, merciless and unrelenting, a force that is better co-operated with than opposed. It is a symbol of those operations of Nature which are more important than any consideration of the individual potencies involved. The mysteries of EAR are behind all those natural disasters and 'acts of God', such as flood, earthquake and volcanic eruption, which destroy the lives of every plant, animal or human that happen to be in the way.

Letter:	QU
Name:	CWEORP
Meaning:	Fire-Stick

CWEORP is an extension of the power of TIR, giving the ability not only to vanquish but to hold onto one's conquests once they are made. It is also concerned with the ability to rule oneself and others and is therefore associated with discipline on all levels, from giving up smoking or going on a diet to the practice of martial arts or a regime of meditation.

Letter:	K
Name:	CALC
Meaning:	Material Well-Being

CALC is a Rune which has the power of drawing into a runic practitioner's life the material conditions he or she would most like to experience. As the requirements will differ in every case, it is hard to predict exactly what the outcome of using this Rune will be. Also it will only work on that desire which holds the greatest appeal to the person for whose good it is invoked. If you want three children *and* the peace and quiet to write your first novel, you must decide which of these you would like to have first. Otherwise the two ambitions will neutralize one another and you will end up doing neither.

Letter: ST
Name: STAN
Meaning: Stone

In discussing SIGEL I have mentioned the idea of trolls and giants being turned into stone. The Teutonic shaman saw stone as an effective way of imprisoning unpleasant or aggressive energies for a considerable period of time, and this Rune was often used as a shield against the negative influences or thought forms of others, both of humans and the gods. The only force against which it is ineffective is that of the WYRD, the three Norns: Fate and Time.

Note that it does not reflect negative energies back to their originator as do some mirror techniques. It simply stops such forces dead in their tracks, at the same time rendering them totally harmless and ineffective.

Letter: hard G
Name: GAR
Meaning: Spear

Like Odin's magic spear, Gungnir, this Rune represents an energy sent forth by the shaman which will find its mark and then return. It is very useful for gathering necessary information at a distance. I frequently use it to check quotations when the local reference library is closed.

Anyone thinking they could use this force to harm another, however, had better think again. The important thing about GAR is that it *returns*; and if one tries to use it for evil, then the rebound can be extremely unpleasant.

Divination Practice
An Astrological Runecast

This runecast will give a good all-round reading, examining every department of the querent's life. It is useful for simply 'looking ahead' when the querent has no specific problem in mind but merely wants to have some understanding of the trends to which he is likely to be subjected over the coming twelve months.

Timing
One year into the future.

Method
Following the instructions given on page 29, select thirteen Runes and lay

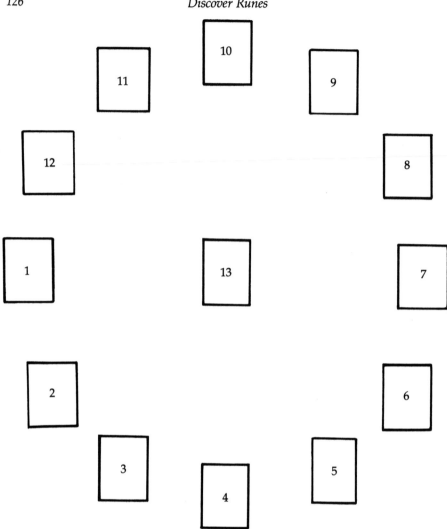

Figure 14: An Astrological Runecast

them out according to Figure 14. These positions represent the twelve 'Houses' of an astrological chart; the twelve divisions of life centred around a personal Rune representing the querent as a totality.

A brief list of what each of the twelve Houses represents appears on page 128. There are some slight differences in the meanings attributed to each House by the old Teutonic star-gazers and those in vogue with modern astrologers. It is not within the scope of this book to explain the logic behind these differences, but I can assure the reader that there are perfectly valid reasons for every association listed on page 128, and I am content to leave each student to reach their own conclusions by experimenting with both systems. Personally, I find the older attributions more reliable.

Read the Runes one by one in relation to the House they are in. Thus, BEORC in the Fifth House (which has to do with children), may signify a birth; in the Sixth House (work or service) it might signify that the querent would do well in catering or hotel work, since BEORC in this House shows a tendency to 'mother' other people. Further examples will be found in those sections of the text that deal with the Runes individually.

The central Rune will show what area of the querent's personality could with profit be expanded or, alternatively, held in check. For instance, with ANSUR in position 13, the querent should trade on their ability to communicate; while NIED in this position suggests that they tend to dwell on the gloomy side of life at the expense of its more optimistic aspects.

List of Houses

First House: The querent's temperament, immediate circumstances, physical stamina and natural abilities.

Second House: The querent's monetary situation and earning capacity.

Third House: Short journeys, letters and communications, mental recreation. The querent's brothers and sisters, subordinates or assistants.

Fourth House: The querent's home, happiness, bodily comforts, property, reputation and education. The querent's mother.

Fifth House: Talent, sustained literary production, physical recreation, speculation, gambling, love affairs, pregnancy, learning, memory, intelligence, further education. The querent's children.

Sixth House: Transient mental and physical ailments, debility, worries, quarrels, enemies, obstacles and impediments to success, gain through service and hard work.

Seventh House: Marriage, partnerships, lawsuits. The querent's spouse or business partner.

Eighth House: Longevity, serious diseases, serious mental distress, clandestine acts, accidents, formidable obstacles to success, troubles to spouse, splitting of partnerships or splits between friends, legacies, money permanently tied up in investments or property.

Ninth House: Good fortune, good luck, long journeys, foreign travel. The querent's spiritual and philosophical outlook. The querent's father.

Tenth House: Success, fame, rank, status. The querent's profession or employment.

Eleventh House: Profit and loss, desires and their fulfilment (or not, as the case may be). The querent's friends and social life.

Twelfth House: Self-undoing, sorrow, loss, separations, imprisonment, hospitalization, fall from position, extravagance, impediments to sexual fulfilment, renunciation and self-sacrifice.

PART TWO
MAGIC

Chapter 9

RUNESCRIPTS

If you have ever wondered why some people are so against the practice of divination, insisting not so much that it is impossible to look into the future as that the power to do so is dispensed by the forces of evil, even the Devil himself, this chapter may throw some light on the subject.

The first thing to be remembered is that the shaman-priests of Germany, Scandinavia, Iceland and Anglo-Saxon Britain were famed not only for their skills in divination but also for their powers as magicians. There is a story recorded by the Venerable Bede, writing in the seventh century AD, that indicates the high esteem in which runic magic was held by the Anglo-Saxons of his day. He tells of a certain soldier who was captured by his enemies and thrown into prison in chains. This man's brother was a Christian who, under the impression that his kinsman was dead, had a series of Masses said for the relief of his soul. According to Bede, every time a Mass was performed the prisoner's fetters flew open. His captors, assuming him to be a runic magician, asked him repeatedly to reveal to them the 'Runes of Unlocking'. All to no avail, the old monk informs us, since the prisoner was being aided by Christian and not pagan magic.

Besides indicating the kind of powers the runic shaman were thought to possess, this account is also interesting for the parallel Bede is at pains to draw between runic magic and Christian magic. The difference between the two (in the eyes of the devout Christian) being that Christian magic is of God and all other magic, by definition, is not. In any religion which accepts only one interpretation of God, all rival cults must of necessity be of the Devil.

Organized religion has never been able entirely to stamp out the practice of either divination or magic. Christianity and Judaism, for instance, are hampered in this respect by the fact that the Bible contains numerous examples of both; magical acts performed by Christ and his followers in the New Testament, or by the Prophets and Patriarchs in the Old, being generally referred to as *miracles*. Popular feeling has always been in favour of divination, and during the past hundred years the predictive arts have made a welcome reappearance in a more scientifically acceptable guise. This has been due mainly to a greater understanding of mankind's inherent psychic abilities, which has itself been the direct result of major breakthroughs in the fields of psychology and psychotherapy.

Magic, on the other hand, because of its accreted associations with Satan, the Black Mass and the Evil Eye, has taken longer to regain its old position. There is, however, no reason to see the concepts of magic and evil as synonymous. Magic can be good and helpful. The Teutonic shaman used it to heal and to bless, to promote fertility and to banish depression and inertia. These were noble aims and the runic magician was generously rewarded for the working of a successful spell.

Creating a Runescript

Magic and divination are two sides of the same coin. This is true of whatever system one is working, but it can perhaps be seen more clearly when dealing with the Runes. As explained in Chapter 2, each of the twenty-four Alphabet Runes represent a facet of one or other of the basic Universal Forces, the total number of which the Teutonic shaman believed to be nine. In divination the placement and combination of these symbols indicates in what direction these basic energies are flowing in the querent's life at any given time. Contrary to what most people think, however, these forces are not immutable. They may be altered or at least significantly deflected by the action (or sometimes the inaction) of the querent. If a reading shows that a querent would be unhappy were they to marry the person with whom they are at present involved, it is an obvious warning. And the querent who chooses to heed that warning will be saving themselves a lot of grief.

But, if the fortuitous layout of the Runes signifies the flow of the Universal Forces as mirrored to the conscious mind by the subconscious mind, then, argued the runic magicians, it must be possible for the conscious mind itself to make contact with these Universal Forces by manipulating the runic symbols used to represent them. In order to accomplish this the conscious mind has only to arrange the symbols so that they are *indicative of the desired result*, and the subconscious mind will reflect this wish or desire back to the Universal Forces, who will then attempt to co-operate with the request *in so far as they are able*.

As far as the runic system is concerned, this manipulation of symbols can be effected in one of two ways. The first method is called *runescript* and is the subject of the present chapter. The second method is called *bindrune* and is dealt with in Chapter 10.

In runescript, the runic magician lines up a group of Runes in such a way that, if he or she found them so associated in a runecast, they would foreshadow or predict the very event desired. Perhaps this process is best illustrated by an example.

Although you should initially work runescripts and bindrunes only on yourself, for the purpose of this illustration we will imagine that we have been asked to prepare a runic talisman for a friend who has been having problems with their love-life. A lot of petty quarrels have sprung up for no apparent reason and there is a general lack of co-operation and harmony in the relationship at present. Thus, the two people concerned need to be brought closer together, and any sense of grievance or disharmony dissolved. So we must ask ourselves which Runes we would expect to see come up in a runecast to indicate a happy and loving relationship. We could be reasonably certain that GEOFU would be prominent in the cast, if only to point out that the problem is mainly concerned with partnership matters. So we can take GEOFU from our runeset and lay it out on our diviner's cloth. Also, FEOH is a helpful Rune for emotional matters of any kind since it indicates the consolidation of a fortunate phase in a love-affair. So we could place FEOH next to GEOFU in the imaginary runecast we are forming.

When there is a disruption in any relationship which has previously been happy and contented, it is generally a sign that, for one reason or another, the lovers have begun to develop in different directions. To correct this trend and incline them to draw closer together again, we can use the Rune KEN, since this Rune is indicative of a new start. This Rune is also beneficial to all romantic aspirations since it denotes reciprocity. And, on top of everything else, it has a strong protective influence.

Because we need to restore the feelings of love and harmony *before* any other improvements can be made, we must make KEN *precede* GEOFU in our imaginary runecast, and not come after it. It is probably a good idea to 'freeze' the mutual regard indicated by KEN so that it cannot diminish or trickle away. So we can place IS, which represents the concept of freezing or holding, immediately after KEN. Finally, we want both parties to be pleased with the results of our magic so we can place WYNN at the end of our line of Runes to signify a happy outcome.

If we felt satisfied that this 'runecast' faithfully reproduced the situation we are being asked to bring about, our next step would be to write it out on a clean slip of white paper, or carve it on a sliver of wood or piece of metal. This would represent our resultant runescript, and Figure 15 shows how it should look. A

Figure 15: A Runescript

runescript is a formalized prayer, a plea to the Universal Forces to reproduce in material terms those conditions symbolically indicated by the grouping of specific Runes in a particular way. If you have learnt the meanings of the Elder Futhark given in Chapters 3 to 7, you should have no trouble in assembling runescripts for any problem that may come your way. Sometimes, however, students are put off by the fact that each Rune has so many meanings. Your experience during divination will have taught you much about what the various combinations of Runes can mean, but if you feel unsure about your own judgement, I have provided a list of those concepts attached to each Rune which are most often utilized in runic magic (see page 142).

Since the English language is written from left to right, it is usual for modern runescripts to follow the same convention. There is no reason, however, why runescripts should not be written in any direction at all. Like Chinese calligraphy or Egyptian hieroglypics, runescripts may be executed from left to right, from right to left, or even upwards or downwards in columns; not to mention alternately forwards and backwards, a formula which is given a special name, Boustrophedon, which means 'like ploughing a field'. Examples of runic scripts written according to all these systems can be found on stone monuments in both Scandinavia and the British Isles.

If, however, you decide to write a runescript from right to left (that is, against the modern convention), you must be sure that you write your Runes *back to front* as well. Figure 16 is the same runescript as that shown in Figure 15 but written from right to left. If you were only to write the order of the Runes backwards, you could end up signifying something very different from what you intended. In the present example you would be freezing (IS) the partnership (GEOFU) before bringing the couple closer together again (KEN); and it might be that you would be drawing them into some formal alliance, such as marriage, while freezing the relationship at its present unsatisfactory level, thus producing an unhappy union entered into for all the wrong reasons.

Figure 16: Runescript Written Right to Left

It is also traditional to form runescripts from odd numbered groups of Runes. There are several exceptions to this rule but wherever possible, the beginner should attempt to follow it. Initially novices in runic magic should confine themselves to combinations of three, five or at the most seven Runes only. Larger groupings can prove unwieldly in the hands of an inexperienced practitioner. Simple requests can be dealt with quite satisfactorily by short groupings, and multiple requests (help me to buy a car, pass my driving test and win the Italian Grand Prix) should be handled one at a time.

In educated circles in the middle ages, magic was referred to as 'occult science', and for this reason the would-be magician should always put him or herself in the position of a scientific experimenter. If you wish to operate as an occult scientist, you should remember that the only person you have a right to practise on is yourself. Until you have gained considerable experience both in the art of divination and in devising runescripts for your own purposes, you should suppress the desire to 'improve' the lives of your friends, especially where this 'improvement' is undertaken without their knowledge or consent. No matter how good or how honourable your intentions, it is not for you to decide what is wrong with anyone else's life for, if your estimation of the situation is awry, you could cause an awful lot of unhappiness to the people concerned. So do be careful how you choose the Runes to make up your runescripts.

The first rule of magic is to use common sense at all times. If you find yourself in an unpleasant or irritating situation, do not begin your runescript with an Increase-Rune such as FEOH or you may find that it is the *problem* you have increased and not your stamina or luck or whatever it was you meant to boost. Neither, in a similar situation, should you commence your runescript with a Holding-Rune, or you will only succeed in holding the situation in its present difficult condition while, at the same time, allowing it neither to improve nor to go away. Likewise, if your intention is to preserve something — a job, a relationship, a state of mind — do not include in your runescript either of the Change-Runes, UR or EOH.

One useful combination to remember for use with all runescripts whose aim is the preservation of an object or an objective is: KEN, IS — *protect* then *freeze*. This ensures that you are preserving something free of negative influences. For, no matter how desirable a situation may appear to you, it should always be assumed that there will be hidden snags of which you are unaware. KEN here acts like the sterilization of the surgeon's instruments prior to an operation, and this Rune should therefore be employed in all preservation magic intended to protect or guard material possessions on the principle that it is better to be safe than sorry.

Runescripts can be carved on wood, scratched on metal, drawn on slips of paper or card, or painted on any suitable surface. If you wish to paint or draw your runescripts in coloured pencil or crayon, the colours to use are: blue on white, blue on lilac, red on white, green on white or dark green on light green. These are combinations of the traditional colours associated with runic magic as mentioned in Chapter 2. Runes carved or scratched onto a wooden or metallic surface may either be painted or left in a state of nature.

Having made your runescript the next step is to consecrate it. Consecration is a subject all to itself and consequently it has a separate section allocated to it in the next chapter. For the present I will continue by explaining what to do with your runescript once it is consecrated.

You can either carry it with you (a purse or a wallet is a good place to keep a runescript) or you can put it in a safe place somewhere around your house. This safe place, wherever it is, should be clean and tidy and out of reach of prying eyes and inquisitive fingers. Some students clear a special place on their dressing tables, while others buy tiny trinket boxes to keep their current runescripts in.

When you have reached the stage where you feel competent enough to make a runescript for someone else, you can give them the runescript and instruct them either to carry it with them or to put it in a safe place of their own devising. Of course, they don't have to be given custody of the runescript at all; some runic magicians prefer to look after their own talismans while waiting for them to do their work.

Legend has it that in order to be effective a runescript intended to influence another person must be handed to them by the runic magician. Personally, I have not found this to be correct, comforting thought though it may be in certain circumstances. In any case it is contradicted by certain other old tales in which the runescript merely hangs over the patient's bed or is buried in the ground at a spot over which they habitually pass. On the other hand, I must admit that some runescripts do seem to work more speedily if the 'personal contact' method is resorted to.

When your runescript has achieved its purpose (always supposing that it was intended to produce a particular finite result), you can either burn it or bury it in the earth. Both are methods of *decomposition* and allow any excess force still retained by the runescript to be released back into the general pool of magical energy from which it was drawn forth in the first place.

In the poems and chronicles of the Norse and Anglo-Saxon peoples, references can be found to the different types of Runes in use by the shaman-magicians at the beginning of the Christian era. These inform us that there were Health-Runes and Healing-Runes (which are not the same thing), Love-Runes, Fertility-Runes, Birth-Runes, Battle-Runes, Victory-Runes, Speech-Runes, Thought-Runes, Weather-Runes and Surf-Runes, not to mention the *yfelruns*: the Cursing-Runes, the Death-Runes and the infamous Ale-, or Taboo-Runes.

Sometimes classification into type signifies a particular *class* of Rune, sometimes a certain *grouping* of Runes is intended. Sometimes the term is applied to all twenty-four Runes of the Elder Futhark, which, in various combinations, are capable of producing a multiplicity of effects. Thus, any of the Alphabet Runes can be used as Weather-Runes depending on the kind of climatic conditions the runic magician deems it necessary to produce. (As I have already explained in the section relating to HAGALL, tampering with the weather was not undertaken lightly, but it was resorted to in specific circumstances, though frequently on a temporary basis only.)

What is remarkable about the above list is how long it is. When one recalls that the Germanic people were reluctant to commit their runic lore to writing, it becomes clear that any record we possess of the uses to which the Runes could be put will represent only the tip of the iceberg. However, because these other uses were not placed on record, they usually need to be recovered by researchers working with the Runes and their tutelary runic deities: Odin, Freyja and the Norns.

Some Examples
Ideally, runescripts (and bindrunes, when we come to them) should be created for the occasion. It is one of the advantages of runic magic that it is intensely personal, that it can induce the Universal Forces to work upon a specific problem in a specific way. But it is this very point which often frightens the novice off, for he or she generally has a great reluctance to design original runescripts. Instead, there is a preference for sticking to proven formulae. These tried and trusted runescripts may have worked admirably for the person for whom they were created, but there is the possibility that they will not be able to produce the same results for any subsequent user because no two individuals will share exactly the same requirements.

This is the reason why runescripts copied from the works of other researchers sometimes fail to produce the results claimed for them. There are, however, certain basic needs and desires which are common to most humans, and runescripts pertaining to these urges can generally be used successfully by almost anyone.

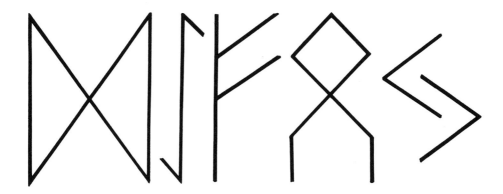

Figure 17: Runescript for Improving Job Prospects

Figure 17, for example, has been used by several of my students to bring about fortunate and progressive changes in their job situations. The first symbol is DEAG, representing (a) a *gradual* change, nothing too drastic, and (b) prosperity — the eventual aim of the runescript. The second Rune is YR to protect the user from making a wrong decision, so that even apparent setbacks can ultimately be turned to one's advantage. The next two Runes, FEOH and OTHEL, form a configuration of their own, meaning, at one level, money to spend plus money in the bank, and at another, a step forward (FEOH) consolidated (OTHEL). The final symbol, JARA, represents a tangible result, an actual reward for previous effort.

For some, this runescript initiates a change of employer, occasionally a change of direction in one's career, while for others it has brought promotion or an acknowledgement of services that had appeared to have been taken for granted. In every case, however, the change has been beneficial and has led to a monetary increase. I am happy, therefore, to release it onto the world at large, confident that it will continue to bring good fortune to its users.

The second example has, likewise, proved itself to be most effective. Figure 18 is a runescript for restoring vitality when one is run down. It may be used as a 'tonic' but is not intended to replace medical aid. If anyone continues to feel run down over a period of time, they should consult a doctor to find out if they are suffering from some vitamin or mineral deficiency. But for those of us who become periodically depleted by the pace at which we are expected to live our lives, this runescript is an excellent corrective.

The first two Runes are for health, success and victory in 'bouncing back'. The third Rune, EOLH, protects the physical body from every kind of harm, internal or external, while ING, the fourth character, represents mental and physical equilibrium. The last Rune, WYNN, also signifies happiness and this refers as much to an untroubled mind, so necessary even to recovery from bodily ills, as to delight at the final result.

The next example (Figure 19) is a different kind of runescript altogether. It is intended to safeguard a computer or typewriter both from breaking down at an inconvenient time and from being stolen. It will not prevent your computer or typewriter from ever going wrong but it will make sure that they do not do so *while in use*. They may go on the blink but you will at least be able to finish what you are doing. The next time you switch the machine on, however, you will probably find that it is out of commission. I have used this script on my own typewriter and computer and can thoroughly recommend it.

The first two Runes are our old friends KEN and IS, protect (this machine) and hold onto it. The Rune OTHEL denotes that what we are wanting to protect is a possession, an object rather than a person. This Rune also signifies mechanical and/or electrical appliances, so it is doing double duty here. (It is no use complaining that the ancient Teutons knew little or nothing about electricity or mechanics. This Rune corresponds to these factors by virtue of its archaic meaning being extended into the present day. Anyone who doubts this can discover the connection for themselves pragmatically by experimentation.)

Figure 18: Runescript for Restoring Vitality

Figure 19: Runescript to Safeguard your Typewriter

The last two Runes indicate what kind of possession it is we wish to protect. RAD and ANSUR are both Mercury-ruled Runes, and Mercury/Odin is the god of communication. RAD is also a symbol of duality and interaction, and can represent the two hands on the keyboard of a typewriter or the working partnership of computer and hacker.

Figure 20 is a runescript intended to strengthen a person's will-power. It contains no Runes to indicate in which direction this will-power is to be used, so it may need a slight adaptation in some cases. The first Rune, EOLH, indicates that the runescript is intended to work on a person rather than a thing. It also shows a new interest forming in the person's mind which hopefully will squeeze out the negative trait we are attempting to displace. Next comes the Anglo-Saxon Rune CWEORP, indicative of discipline and self-control. The third symbol is MANN, which endows one with a detached and pensive frame of mind. This Rune ensures that the user of this script will think out what he or she is doing, how their negative actions are ultimately damaging their chances of living a better, fuller life. PEORTH brings hidden resources to light, particularly those signified by the following two Runes, KEN and TIR. Both these runes are ruled by Mars and depict a new project energetically undertaken (KEN) and a decision stoutly defended (TIR). The last Rune, IS, holds the powers of Mars which would otherwise quickly disperse.

For those individuals who feel they would like to alter a negative character-trait but who also feel a strong pull in the opposite direction, a reluctance to free themselves from the shackles of habit, the Rune MANN should be changed to DAEG. This will enable a better attitude to the problem to develop. Often a different viewpoint emerges which shows up the habit as a genuine stumbling block or source of ill-health and not merely an attractive intellectual concept.

Purists may complain at finding an Anglo-Saxon Rune in a runescript line-up. However, the last example (Figure 21), taken from the Anglo-Saxon poem *The Husband's Message* shows an early English runescript which also mixes the symbols. In my opinion this runecast was for success, especially in fishing or travelling overseas. It was probably deliberately misinterpreted to divest it of its magical implications so that it could continue to be used on ships and boats on a plea of sentimental attachment, thus escaping the censure of the Church.

It reads quite clearly. SIGEL, success, but not combined with TIR, so armed combat is not intended. RAD, travel, EAR, across the ocean. WYNN, a traveller — particularly one whose work causes them to travel — gains happiness and (DAEG) prosperity. Sometimes the last letter is given as MANN, which would mean 'in the company of others, as part of a group effort, etc.'

For the conventional, scholastic interpretation of this runescript see R.W.V. Elliott's *Runes*, page 73. Apart from the meanings allocated to the first two Runes, this translation is actually very close to the esoteric one. The poem to which this runescript is appended might lead a researcher in a particular direction but the magical significance of the symbols is crystal clear, even using

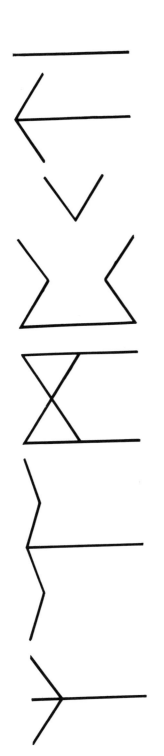

Figure 20: Runescript for Strengthening Will-Power

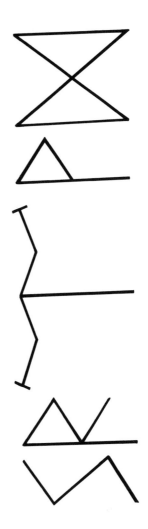

Figure 21: Runescript taken from *The Husband's Message*

the association ascribed to the Runes by Elliott himself in Chapter 5 of his book.

Short List of Magical Meanings of the Elder Futhark

ᚠ

Increase of wealth, increase of property, protection of valuables; to consolidate an emotional relationship, or sometimes to hasten an affair on to its next stage.

ᚢ

To draw new circumstances into a person's life, to initiate new conditions without being specific about what those conditions should be. Thus, one may work to get a new house but may *not* stipulate that it must be 7, Acacia Avenue. (See EOH.)

ᚦ

Protection from one's own folly. Luck — to be used in situations where you are unable to influence results yourself in any way, i.e. for an operation, where the outcome is partly due to the skill of the surgeon and partly in the lap of the gods.

ᚨ

For all matters connected with education and communication: learning, scholarship, teaching, negotiations, debate, public speaking, public appearances, writing. To instil confidence in 'exam' situations whether GCSEs, job interviews, auditions, driving tests or quiz programmes.

ᚱ

Safety and comfort in travel. Satisfaction in all things associated with transport: luggage, car, aeroplane, bicycle.

ᚲ

Protection of valuables, physical well-being, self-confidence, positivity; fresh starts; stability in relationships.

ᚷ

Harmony, concord, all things to do with partnerships both business and emotional; mental and physical equilibrium.

ᚹ

Fulfilment in almost any area, but especially in love or career matters. Successful results of travel.

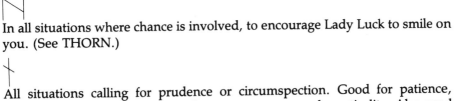

In all situations where chance is involved, to encourage Lady Luck to smile on you. (See THORN.)

All situations calling for prudence or circumspection. Good for patience, determined effort, long-term goals, common sense and practicality. Also used in love magic to ginger-up a relationship that is taking too long to get off the ground.

To freeze, to preserve, to hold matters as they are, or as the preceding Runes have encouraged them to become.

Wherever a tangible result is required in exchange for expenditure of money, time or trouble. The tangibility of the result need not be financial, it can take the form of kudos, honour or preferment. Help in legal matters.

Protection, to remove obstacles or to miraculously transmute them into stepping-stones to success.

Legacies, investments, speculation, gambling, all psychological problems. The finding of lost things.

Protection against the evil thoughts and activities of others. Promotes all relationships founded on friendship rather than physical attraction. Helpful for all pursuits in which you are required to renounce one opportunity in order to take up another, especially in academic and artistic areas.

Health, physical strength, clear thinking, self-confidence.

Victory through struggle, powers of recuperation, enthusiasm, for all situations involving conflict or competition.

All domestic affairs: everything concerning spouse, children, family home. Birth, matters to do with children generally.

To bring about specific changes, usually changes denoted by other Runes in the runescript. Good for all modes of travel: land, sea or air. EOH would be used to bring about changes within an existing relationship, or within a pre-defined career structure, whereas UR would tend to produce a totally new relationship or precipitate a complete change of career, and is connected with opportunities not known to the querent at the time of making the runescript or bindrune.

The goodwill and assistance of others. Fortunate for all joint or group activities, or for anything intended for the benefit or advancement of mankind. Also, mental ingenuity and inventive ability.

Conception, psychic matters, intuition, inner awareness, artistic endeavour, painting, musicianship, acting, all forms of education which are allied to the imagination. Teaching, guidance.

To bring something to a satisfactory conclusion, to hold or 'fix' a conclusion so as to prevent the benefits accrued either from draining away or being appropriated by others.

Financial increase, good for changes of attitude, new resolutions, re-evaluation of one's outlook or position.

Protection of possessions, heirlooms, antiques, house and land. Encourages a down-to-earth attitude and a practical approach to the problems of life. Good for long-term investments, care of the elderly, physical labour, gardening, building, repair work, etc.

Divination Practice
The Celtic Cross

This runecast is adapted from the well-known Tarot spread of the same name, and illustrates the principle that layouts designed for use with the Tarot can be readily converted into runecasts so long as the original spread contains no more than twenty-five placements.

There are several versions of the Celtic Cross, each varying slightly in the allocation of meanings to the ten positions and the order in which the cards are laid out — particularly those used to form the Cross itself. I have chosen a layout which differs somewhat from that published in *The Tarot Workbook*; but if you are familiar with that pattern, or with any other, I would advise you to stick to the method you already know. There is no need to confuse yourself by learning two contradictory systems.

The only difference between the runecast and the Tarot spread from which it has been adapted are that it uses no Significator to represent the querent; and, because the Runes do not lie happily across one another, the Rune which represents 'that which crosses the querent', is laid *beneath* the first Rune and not *across* it as in the Tarot version. These considerations aside, the runecast works in just the same way as does the Tarot spread.

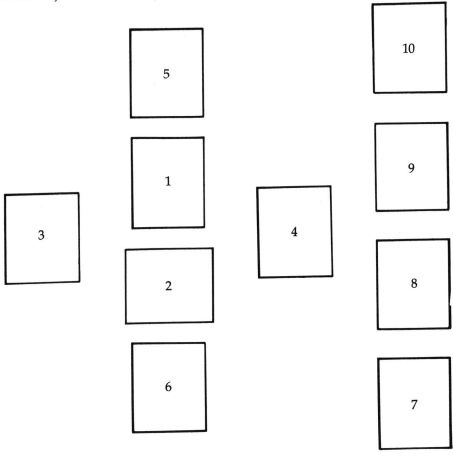

Figure 22: The Celtic Cross

Method

Following the directions on page 29, select ten Runes at random and lay them out according to the pattern shown in Figure 22 (or in the order you are used to).

Position 1:   The problem, or that aspect of life most likely to give trouble.

Position 2:   The main obstacle to progress. Read this Rune as if it revealed its most negative face.

Position 3:   Past influences.

Position 4:   Future influences.

Position 5:   What ambitions or ideals motivate the querent.

Position 6:   What the querent can (or sometimes, should) do to influence events themselves.

Position 7:   What factors in the querent's psychological make-up have bearing on the problem.

Position 8:   What factors in the querent's environment have relevance to the situation.

Position 9:   The querent's hopes (positive Rune) or fears (negative Rune).

Position 10: Final Result — *but tempered by the Rune in position 4.*

Chapter 10

BINDRUNES

The rules governing the formation of bindrunes are much the same as those governing the construction of runescripts. The main difference between the two techniques lies in their physical appearance. Instead of being written out one after another as in a sentence, bindrunes are formed by making an overlay of the constituent Runes, and it is to this peculiarity that bindrunes owe their name. They are not so called because they are used to *bind* any object or person to the runic magician, or to anyone else, though this is commonly thought to be the case.

The advantages that bindrunes have over runescripts are purely practical. On the one hand, a bindrune takes up far less room than a runescript and is thus to be preferred where space is at a premium; while on the other hand, the superimposition of one Rune over another often produces an attractive or unusual composite symbol which can be displayed quite openly without anyone ever suspecting its magical connotations. This last consideration is usually well to the fore where the runic talisman is of a perpetual or long-term nature, such as one giving protection from ill-health or physical attack, and where the person for whom the talisman has been created would prefer, for whatever reason, to carry the item on them.

The one disadvantage to using a bindrune is that it cannot generally be made to contain any more than five runic symbols at most, and must therefore be limited to very simple requests. However, since most of humanity's needs are essentially simple (despite the fact that the conscious mind will try to make them seem infinitely complicated) this fact should not cause you any sleepless nights. In fact, it is good practice in analysing one's problems to be forced to pare each one down to its bare essentials in this way. This is not such a difficult task, especially (as I have already mentioned with regard to the formation of runescripts) if the various stages of the problem are taken one at a time.

The number of Runes in a bindrune needs to be limited to a maximum of five because it is important that each character should retain its own individual expression while at the same time blending in with the unique vibration of the newly created sigil. If you try making a bindrune out of the whole of the Elder Futhark you will soon see what I mean. Some Runes — notably MANN and possibly TIR — stand out clearly, while others, such as IS and LAGU, become lost in the overall pattern.

It is important when constructing a bindrune that the finished symbol be as balanced and harmonious to the eye as possible. This is not the same as saying that it should be *symmetrical*, though it is surprising how many bindrunes do end up exhibiting this characteristic. Because balance is such a vital requirement, the rule that all Runes must face in one direction only, which applies in the case of runescripts, is ignored. After all, a bindrune is not being written in any particular direction since it is the calligraphic equivalent of running on the spot. A simple example will show how this principle is to be used in order to achieve a balanced symbol.

Suppose you wanted to make a bindrune to help yourself through your 'A' Levels in Economics. You would need to combine ANSUR (for success in examinations) with FEOH (ruling all aspects of money and provision). In this case a balanced design can be formed by placing the two Runes back to back (Figures 23 and 24). Either Rune can be made to face in the 'normal' direction, as the illustration makes clear. Which version you select will depend on which design has the greatest appeal to you.

I would suggest that you make several attempts at any bindrune you would like to have a go at, trying all sorts of combinations and variations, and then choose the one that seems to you most pleasing to the eye. Although this may seem like an unnecessary duplication of effort the first couple of times you try it, it becomes easier with practice, and the resultant bindrune is usually well worth the extra work involved.

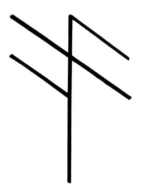
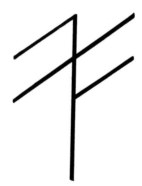

Figure 23: Bindrune to Help With   Figure 24: Bindrune to Help With
            Exams   Exams, Mirror Image

Although you should be careful not to eclipse the identity of any of the individual Runes from which a bindrune is constructed, it is a curious fact that when the final sigil is completed, 'hidden' Runes applicable to the problem under review can often be discerned within the finished design. In Figures 23 and 24 a NIED appears, indicative of perseverance and success through hard work; and there is also a foreshortened YR, which has the meanings of approach to a goal, difficulties averted, and protection – all of which would be most helpful in a bindrune intended to help with the passing of an exam.

Bindrunes possess one further peculiarity that runescripts do not and that is the Earthing Line. This is a horizontal bar placed at the bottom of the bindrune, usually between the 'feet' of any Rune not based on a single vertical stroke. The Earthing Line is a fixative, it holds things in position. In many ways it is like the Holding-Rune IS which, as we have seen, tends to lose its identity when overlaid by other letters. The Earthing Line, however, does not exactly parallel the function of the Holding-Rune, for it also indicates a material or physical result, and thus has certain affinities with the Rune JARA, a time for harvest. The Teutonic name for the Earthing Line has not come down to us, so far as I am aware, but my researches show that the corresponding planet is our own Earth, and the equivalent Nordic goddess is Jord, a type of Earth Goddess and the mother of Thor.

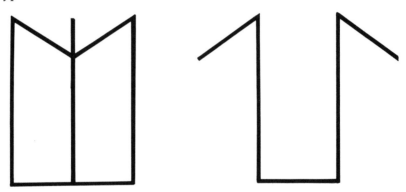

Figure 25: Bindrune showing an Earthing Line

Figure 26: Two LAGUs Joined by an Earthing Line

Figure 25 shows a bindrune for protection, luck and guidance in a new job. It is formed from EOH (a change of job), EOLH (protection for a person) and the Earthing Line (material result). The Earthing Line can also be used to join two identical Runes based on a single vertical stroke and which would lose their individual characteristics simply by being placed back to back. For instance, Figure 26 shows two LAGUs joined by an Earthing Line. If these Runes had been set back to back, they would have formed a single TIR — and that would not have been what was intended at all. This bindrune was originally designed as a pendant for a mother who wanted to teach her daughter at home rather than send her to school. One LAGU represents the mother/teacher and the other the daughter/pupil. It was imperative to keep the two LAGUs separate, otherwise an intrusive force, masculine and competitive, would have been invoked, and the mother particularly wanted to avoid the competitive aspect inherent in much formal education.

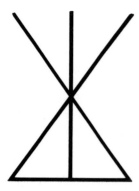
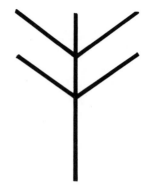

Figure 27: Bindrune to Preserve a Love   *Figure 28:* Bindrune Containing a
Relationship   'Hidden' Rune EOLH

Another example showing the use of both IS and the Earthing Line can be found in Figure 27. This is a bindrune for preserving a love-relationship. It is based on GOEFU (for love), the Earthing Line (for a tangible result) and IS (to preserve). One word of warning about this sigil, however. This bindrune should only be used to preserve a relationship which is *already* happy and contented; it cannot be used to improve the quality of your love-life, either by encouraging a new romance to materialize or by dispelling the problems and conflicts which may have arisen in your current affair. In the former case you would be advised to use two FEOHs back to back, as shown in Figure 28, which fortuitously contains the 'hidden' Rune EOLH (a new friendship which may lead to romance); while in the latter case, you could design a runescript along the lines of the example given in Chapter 9 and shown in Figure 15 on page 133.

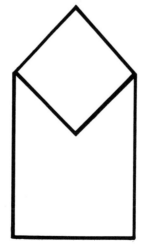

Figure 29: Bindrune With a Dominant ING

Sometimes one Rune may be given greater emphasis in a bindrune by being drawn much larger than any of the others, as in Figure 29. This bindrune was designed for a family emigrating to Canada, and the Rune ING had been made to dominate the pattern because of its associations with finality, one door closing and another opening, thus defining the type of change and movement delineated by the Rune EOH.

It is also permissible to use alternative characters from the other Futharks in order to maintain visual harmony. In fact, the introduction of a cursive variant frequently enlivens and refreshes an otherwise dull and static symbol. Take Figure 30: it is a bindrune for good luck, especially in gambling and speculation, and is composed of the symbol for HAGALL taken from the Younger Futhark and the cursive version of THORN as used in some areas of Britain in Anglo-Saxon times. The softer outline of the rounded THORN makes it a more artistically successful sigil than would otherwise have been the case, as comparison with Figure 31, the rectilinear version, shows.

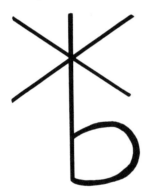 

Figure 30: Bindrune Made up from Different Futharks

Figure 31: The Rectilinear Version of Figure 30

Finally, unlike runescripts, bindrunes may occasionally contain other, non-alphabetic Runes. This, of course, is advanced work because it is necessary to have gained a thorough understanding of Teutonic mythology and symbology before one can even begin to design this type of composite sigil. I mention the process only because there are bindrunes of this type about, on sale at Festivals and Fayres and from certain occult suppliers, and I feel that it is better to explain the principles by which such glyphs are formed, however briefly, than to leave the matter dark with mystery.

Figure 32 is one such bindrune, of Icelandic origin, for attracting love to its possessor. I have chosen this sigil because it illustrates several of the points just covered in a simple and clearly demonstrable way. First, it is based on an alternative of the Rune ING (Figure 33), a symbol of fertility, particularly male fertility. Secondly, the Rune has been made cursive. And thirdly, a Symbol Rune representing the female sexual organ (as ING here represents the male sexual organ) has been added to the arrangement. The whole is thus an

Figure 32: An Icelandic Bindrune   *Figure 33:* The Rectilinear Version of ING in Figure 32

obvious and graphic representation of the physical act of love. This example also proves that, for all their apparent sophistication and complexity, the runic formulae remain firmly rooted in the primitive practices of sympathetic magic.

Old Teutonic Bindrunes
There is another method of forming bindrunes once much favoured by the Teutonic tribes of the Continent but which has fallen out of favour in modern times. This system uses as a base either the Rune GEOFU or the Rune NIED, adding other, smaller Runes to the extremities of the central symbol. The total number of Runes used in this type of bindrune is generally five: one basal Rune with one Rune attached to each 'leg'. Five is, of course, an *odd* number and all odd numbers are considered as being magically potent in the runic system.

These bindrunes are generally for love matters, to attract or hold love. GEOFU is a symbol for partnership (engagement, marriage, sexual union, etc.), and is thus a logical choice for a love talisman, but it may seem odd that NIED should be such a prominent feature of runic love magic. The answer to this paradox lies in the meaning of the word 'nied'. Usually translated *need* or sometimes *necessity*, it also has the meaning *compulsion*. Once again, this does NOT mean that this Rune can be used to compel one person to fall in love with another, for love cannot be commanded. What this type of bindrune will do, however, is to prod a shy or tardy lover into making a declaration of affection. In a culture in which the man has to do the asking and runs the risk of being rejected by so doing, there is often great reluctance to place oneself in so vulnerable a position. In order to overcome this reluctance, the girl who knew a little about runic lore would make a bindrune love-charm for herself; or, if she did not trust her own magical powers, she could commission a runic magician to make one for her.

An example of this type of old Teutonic bindrune based around the Rune NIED is shown in Figure 34. Perhaps it is an indication of the way times have

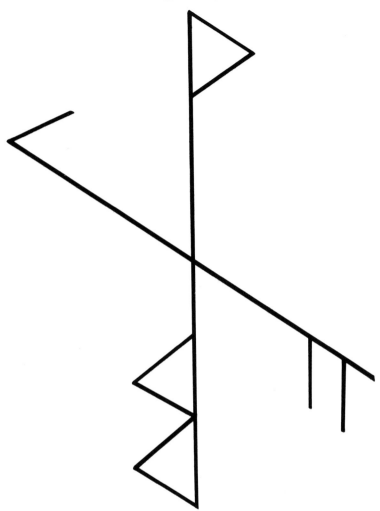

Figure 34: A Teutonic Bindrune

changed, and of the effect that the feminist movement is having on society, that I am more often asked to design this kind of talisman for men than for women. Be that as it may, the symbol in Figure 34 is for a man, and is intended to elicit a positive response, either verbal or physical, from the woman in his life. This is *not* a bindrune for drawing an eligible partner into your sphere of influence — for that purpose a quite different set of symbols must be used. Nor will it work the other way around, to encourage a man to propose to a woman that they should marry or live together. The symbols around the central NIED reading clockwise are: WYNN, for happiness; FEOH, for progress in a love affair; BEORC, for domestic bliss and also as indicative of a celebration within the family; and LAGU, because the person to be chivied is a woman.

By now you should know enough about what each Rune signifies to be able to adapt this example to your own needs. You can change it so that it is suitable for use by a woman, or so that it will attract a congenial mate into the life of the person for whom it is made. There is no need to be afraid to experiment with this type of bindrune as it is practically foolproof. Either it will work in the way intended, in which case you have nothing to worry about, or nothing at all will happen since, by inept handling, the forces concerned are merely cast back into the pool of Universal Energies from which they were originally drawn forth. This occurs because, in this method, no Rune is considered to be in reverse even where this appears to be the case i.e. as with BEORC in Figure 34. These bindrunes are therefore ideal for the novice to practise on and, for this reason, I feel it is a shame that they have fallen into disuse in recent times.

Consecration

Before describing how consecration is effected, it is probably a good idea to say what consecration *is*.

Occult philosophy maintains that energy in its most subtle form can be passed from one object to another. This is the explanation for much spiritual healing that is performed, especially the type known as 'the laying on of hands'. Spiritual healing is the transference of subtle energies from one animate object (the healer) to another (the patient). But it is also possible to pass energy from an animate object to an inanimate object. In the case of consecration, the animate object would be the runic magician and the inanimate object the slip of paper or piece of wood or metal bearing the runescript or bindrune petition.

Now, animate objects circulate and process their own natural energy fairly rapidly, which is why they need constantly to replenish their energy levels by frequent intakes of nutrition in the form of food and drink which can then be converted into fresh energy. On the other hand, inanimate objects are processing energy at such a slow rate that it is almost immeasurable. This is the view according to occult philosophy, and I suppose the scientific view to be much the same since modern physics intimates that even solid matter is simply a way of perceiving energy.

Because inanimate objects use up their own energy so slowly, there is nothing for them to do with any excess energy deposited within them but (a) store it up, or (b) pass it on. What actually happens is a combination of the two processes. The inanimate object retains the energy channelled into it, but releases infinitesimally minute pulses of that energy into the atmosphere at regular, though widely spaced intervals. Thus, it acts rather like a distress beacon, bleeping out its message into the air-waves, waiting to be heard and acted upon. This is a useful analogy, for it is exactly the way in which a consecrated runescript or bindrune behaves.

Consecration also implies a 'setting apart'. This is why, generally, any item used for runic magic is put in a special place, segregated from all mundane artifacts. For the same reason, no magical tool should ever have been used previously for any other purpose. There are a few exceptions to this guideline. For instance: when a runescript (or bindrune) is etched or painted directly onto the object it is meant to influence or protect, such as a car or typewriter. In this case the consecrated article cannot be set apart — but the runescript (or bindrune) usually is, either by being placed on some part of the item where it will not attract attention, or by being 'disguised' as an innocuous symbol or pattern.

Consecration is effected most easily by means of the imaginative faculty. It *can* be accomplished by pure faith, but this is a rather advanced technique facilitated by having received proof that the first method actually works. I find the best way to perform consecration is to place the slip of paper (or whatever it is that the runescript or bindrune is written on) on the diviner's cloth either on the floor or on a low table, and then to stand facing it in the ancient Teutonic invoking position — arms spread out and reaching upwards, with the head thrown back so that the body forms a shape like the letter Y (or the letter EOLH in the Elder Futhark).

If you assume this stance, after a few minutes you will begin to feel a tingling sensation building up in the palms of your hands which will then move slowly down your arms and accumulate in the area of your solar plexus. This is the old Teutonic way of drawing energy from the atmosphere, which is itself impregnated with the Life Force. This Life Force is in the safe-keeping of the gods, though it is not their property and they cannot prevent it from being accumulated and utilized by anyone who knows how to do so.

Allow this energy to build up for two or three minutes (as a beginner you may have to devote as much as five minutes to this exercise in order to create a really tangible force-field within yourself). Then lower your hands and place them, palms downwards, over the item you intend to consecrate. Now, the energy that has built up around your solar plexus will be felt to pass *down* your arms and out through the palms of your hands into the runescript or bindrune talisman. You may not in the initial stages feel the energy passing out through your palms but you will certainly feel it disperse from the chest area and move down your arms. Don't worry if you are unable to follow the path the energy takes all the way to the piece of paper, wood or metal you are attempting to consecrate. Simply accept that, if the energy has shifted from your solar plexus, it must have gone somewhere and, since these subtle energies are manipulated by mind-power, or *intention*, what is more natural than that the energy has relocated itself at the place where you intended it to go?

It is a good idea, when standing in the invoking posture, to state your reasons for wanting to accumulate the energy, and to call upon the appropriate god-force, either from the Nordic/Teutonic pantheon or from some other pantheon with which you are familiar, as this helps to ensure that the energies built up are of a sympathetic vibration to the type of talisman you are working on. When the energy has dissipated, thank the gods (or Universal Forces) for their co-operation. Though the gods are not human beings, they are sentient and in many ways respond just like humans to appeals, slights, praise, or being taken for granted. It was for this reason that almost every mythological system depicted gods and goddesses with the bodies of men and women.

After consecration, the runescript or bindrune may be retained until it has done its work, after which the excess energy still held within it should be released in the manner described at the end of Chapter 9. Some talismans, such as those for protecting a person or a relationship, will be more or less perpetual (as far as the span of human life is concerned at any rate). This type of talisman is best worn or carried upon the person and, so long as the consecration has been performed correctly, it should not need to be reconsecrated at any time. The 'trapped' energy leaks away so slowly that a properly charged artefact can still be active centuries after the death of its creator.

If you come into possession of any item which you suspect has been consecrated at any time in its history, wrap it in cooking foil (I am all for using twentieth century technology) shiny side inwards and bury it in the earth from one new moon to the next. You may also do this with any metallic talismans you have made yourself and which you are loath to melt down — a rather drastic method of *decomposition* for an item which probably has both artistic merit and sentimental value. This method of deconsecration removes any residual energies remaining in the artefact concerned but preserves the talisman itself from decay or material damage so that it may still be used as an ornament either around the house or attached to a necklace or bracelet.

Divination Practice
The Gate of Heaven

This is a very versatile runecast. The Gate of Heaven can be used when the querent has no specific problem, but simply wants to know what trends to expect over the coming twelve-month period. It can also be used to examine the development and outcome of any situation, so long as that situation stands a chance of being resolved within one year.

Timing
One year into the future, with some indication of the present position.

Method
Lay out the Runes face downwards on your diviner's cloth, swirl, and set them out in the pattern shown in Figure 35. (In the traditional version of this runecast, the Runes are laid out slightly differently, i.e. with all the bases facing inwards, but I have found that students using this system easily become confused as to whether a Rune is reversed or not.) It is not essential that the Runes are laid out in the numerical sequence indicated in Figure 35, which is

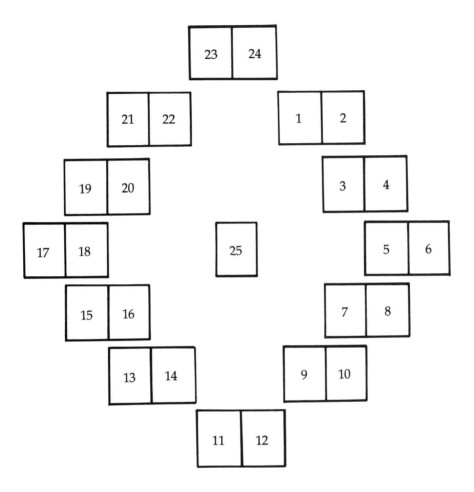

Figure 35: The Gate of Heaven

the order in which the Runes are *interpreted*. It is only important that the querent forms the *pattern* of twelve pairs around a central Rune. However, unless you provide them with some form of template, you will find that most querents will prefer to lay out the Runes sequentially rather than build up the pattern in a haphazard fashion.

Turn over the central Rune. This indicates the general tone of the reading. If it is a negative Rune, you may prefer not to make any comment to the querent at this point — and it is better to hold your peace than to say: 'Well, this is going to be a really lousy twelve months!' — in which case you should pass swiftly on to the next stage.

Examine the Runes in position 1 and 2. This pair usually indicate what it is that is worrying the querent, or it may show which area of life will most concern them during the coming year. The Runes in positions 13 and 14, opposite the first pair, will often be illuminating too, and can be read at this point as relating to the present, or to the recent past.

Read all the pairs in order, working clockwise around the circle. Try to build up a consecutive story as this helps your querent to see their life as having order and meaning. When you reach Runes 13 and 14, you will need to read them again. This time, however, they must be treated as part of your 'consecutive story' and interpreted so that they fit into the unfolding scenario. Occasionally, a reading will not be consecutive, but will consist of two (or even three) themes weaving in and out of one another. It is best to practise reading on one theme only, taking your cue from the Runes in positions 1, 2 and 25, before venturing into the deeper waters of multiple-thread readings.

A non-consecutive reading that seems jarring to your intuitive faculty can often indicate a flaw in the querent's psychology. Either they do not give one project a fair run before charging off on some other enterprise, or they have sunk into a negative mental state and could well be in need of professional help. However, you will need to be quite experienced as a reader before you are able to distinguish between a reading that 'won't come right' and one that indicates an imbalance in the querent.

You can judge nearly enough when important events are likely to occur by counting the first pair of Runes as the month in which the reading takes place, the second pair as the following month, and so on. Thus, for a reading made in May, the Runes EOH reversed and RAD in positions 5 and 6 (the third month) would indicate that the querent would be travelling abroad in July. The first pair of Runes represent the month in which the reading takes place, even if there is only one day of that month left to run. This is because the Runes in positions 1 and 2 have reference to the immediate past as much to the present or future.

When you have read all around the circle, read the central Rune again in the light of the rest of the reading. Usually, this Rune will offer the querent some advice as to how to proceed during the year, or what attitude it would be best to adopt. Even negative Runes here will be found to have something constructive to say, such as: 'Bide your time'; 'Change your plans and you will succeed'; 'Don't throw good money after bad'; and so on.

Chapter 11

THE RUNES AND OTHER SYMBOL SYSTEMS

Nordic Mythology and Other Mythologies

The runic system of magic and divination is only one of many such systems. (Astrology is another, though few astrologers know about, or would even care to acknowledge, the esoteric aspect of their art.) It is usual to define the runic system as the 'Norse Tradition'; but there is also a Celtic tradition, a Graeco-Roman tradition, an Egyptian tradition and, since the time of the 'World Religions', a Christo-Judaic and an Islamic tradition. All these tributaries flow together to form that raging torrent commonly known as the Western Esoteric Tradition.

A question I am often asked is: 'Why are there so many systems still in use within the Western Esoteric Tradition? Why have they not all been welded into one syncretic system?' The answer lies in part in an ancient Hindu saying, 'The paths to God are as many as the breaths of Man'. What this means is that each person has their own path to God and that each path will, of necessity, be different. The Hindus used the symbol of a wheel to illustrate this proverb, pointing out that, like the spokes of a wheel, some of these paths may *appear* diametrically opposed. However, if their journeys are followed from rim to hub, all spokes will be found to share the same eventual destination.

When students first come for training in the Western Esoteric Tradition, they are usually discovered to have an affinity with one or other of the many sub-traditions of which it is comprised, and it is in this tradition that they are initially instructed. This selection is not imposed upon them from without, it is made unconsciously by the student themselves, for generally speaking, students are drawn to those Schools which offer the type of training most suited to their present philosophical and psychological requirements. Students coming into contact with any School teaching a system with which they feel themselves to be incompatible or which seems uncongenial to them should decline entry and continue their search for a spiritual haven in other waters.

Another point which seems to be a constant source of perplexity to students is this: Since there are so many systems, all of them sound and efficient after their fashion, how can one ever hope to master them all? To which the short answer is, 'One can't'. Students should take up that system which seems most congenial to them and master it to the best of their abilities. They may then move on to examine other systems, at which point they will discover that, whatever grade they hold in their own tradition, an equivalent grade is automatically conferred upon them in all corresponding traditions.

I am not talking here of the grades of the conventional 'lodge system'. Useful as this may be during an initial training period, it is no true measure of a person's actual standing as an occultist. The only genuine yardstick here is that of *function*: can a person invoke the Universal Forces? direct them? dispel them? The student/initiate who can do these things in one system can do it in all of them, it only being necessary for him or her to form a rapport with the mythological personifications allotted by the previously unexplored tradition to the Universal Forces, which in this respect represent 'constants' or 'givens'.

Some mythologies, however, may prove more difficult to come to terms with than others. For instance: Norse magic, like Egyptian magic, does not correspond directly to either Greek, Roman or Hebraic magic, and Murry Hope has some interesting things to say on the suitability of the different systems to various psychic temperaments in her instructive *Practical Egyptian Magic* (Aquarian Press, 1984). The Greek philosophers were the first real thinkers of the Western World; the Romans unified large tracts of Europe, Asia Minor and the near East, and thus facilitated the propagation of knowledge; while the Jews provided the religious background to Christianity, which became the first 'world religion' of the West. Consequently, the ways of thought common to the Greeks, the Romans and the Jews appear to be those most accessible to the natives of those countries where the cultural ethos is predominantly European in flavour.

In Greek magic, Zeus is the king of the gods, the father of gods and men, and is the equivalent of the Roman Jupiter. This concept can, in turn, be comprehended by the Christian mind in the form of God the Father, to whom the Paternoster is addressed, while in the Judaic system, this aspect of Jehovah's power is named El. Alas, not all traditions dovetail so readily one into the other. It is sometimes imperative to have a good understanding of the racial, historical and sociological background of a particular mythology in order fully to appreciate its finer points.

In the Norse pantheon, for example, Odin is called the All-Father, which would seem to associate him with the Jupiter force, though almost every other attribute he possesses — his magical powers, his protection of travellers, his guardianship of the alphabet, his capacity to riddle and deceive — casts him in the role of Mercury. This apparent discrepancy is explained by the fact that, while the Greeks, in successive invasions, conquered and settled the ancient land of Hellas, the Teutons remained an essentially nomadic people right up to the time of the Vikings and beyond. Thus the chief god of the Greeks personified law, order and the positive virtues of the Establishment while the Teutons placed themselves under the protection of a more free-wheeling and even somewhat anarchic deity.

It is due to the fact that today even the so-called Anglo-Saxon races have lost the ability to perceive the realities of life from the same philosophical or mythological standpoint as their ancestors did, that it is often easier for them to access the archetypal energies of the Universal Forces via one of the allied and complementary systems with which the Western Esoteric Tradition abounds.

In my opinion, the system to which the Runes bear the closest correspondence is the Celtic tradition. The Celts come from the same racial family as the Teutons of which they represent an earlier migratory wave. The Celts were constantly pushed westwards by the conquest and expansion of the Germanic tribes and the two races were near neighbours for considerable periods both on the Continent and in the British Isles. Thus, many parallel myths are to be found in the literature of both cultures. The story of Sigurd who acquires wisdom by sucking the finger he has burnt when touching the heart of a dragon he has been set to roast, is the same myth as that of Gwiddion who, in the Welsh version of the story, burns his finger while watching over the Cauldron of Inspiration. The similarities are even closer in the Irish tale of Math ap Mathonwy who burnt a finger whilst roasting the Salmon of Inspiration for his master.

Due to the geographical dispersion of the Celts, there developed three interlinked sub-traditions: the Irish, the Welsh and the Scottish. At the present time, however, none of these are in a very cohesive or accessible condition because, in the main, they have been ignored by British and American scholarship in favour of classical literature and mythology. Only the initiates of the Celtic Mystery Schools have a genuine understanding of these traditions and, until recently, none of these has seen fit to make their teachings public.

The Runes and the Arthurian Cycle

For the runic investigator, however, by far the closest set of correspondences are to be found in a rather surprising collection of tales, those concerning King Arthur and the Knights of the Round Table. Each of the twenty-four Runes of the Elder Futhark corresponds to a person or incident in the Mort D'Arthur, though it is not necessary for one to be steeped in Sir Thomas Mallory's great work in order to be able to make the identifications; a purely rudimentary knowledge of the legends will suffice.

Merlin, for instance, is represented by ANSUR, the Rune particularly associated with Odin. Like Odin, Merlin was a great magician and shape-shifter. And, again like Odin, Merlin was doomed to go to his rest at the appointed time, for all his magic powers, helpless to prevent the cataclysm that was to follow. Merlin's pupil, variously called Vivien or Nimue, is represented by the negative aspect of the Rune LAGU, whilst its positive powers are exemplified by that mysterious being, the Lady of the Lake.

King Arthur himself is represented by the fiery Rune KEN in both its aspects, signifying that he would gain everything i.e. the kingship of Britain (upright Rune), and lose everything (reversed Rune). His Queen, Guinevere, whose love for Sir Lancelot sowed the seeds of destruction for the Company of the Table Round, corresponds to GEOFU, a Rune which pays more attention to emotional fulfilment than to considerations of life and limb.

Of the Knights of the Round Table, Sir Gawain is represented by DAEG, a solar Rune. It was said of Gawain that his strength increased in the morning and decreased after noon, and that whenever he was plunged into water it hissed and gave off steam; so the symbolism seems to be most appropriate.

Lancelot, 'the best Knight in the world' as Mallory calls him, is represented by RAD. This may seem a strange choice for such a renowned warrior but it has to do with the fact that RAD indicates anything which has two sides to it, and this perfectly describes the nature of Lancelot which was incomplete without either an opponent, a companion or a lover. The type of person denoted by RAD is rarely if ever found in absolute charge of anything; their need for someone to share it all with them is too great for that. On the other hand, they do make loyal and reliable seconds-in-command. In Arthur, Lancelot finds an alter-ego, a twin soul that he can honour and admire, while in Guinevere he finds love of a very different kind.

RAD in reverse represents a difficult choice, and that is exactly what Lancelot is faced with when he realizes what his true feelings towards Guinevere really are. In the runic alphabet, KEN (Arthur) stands between GEOFU (Guinevere) and RAD (Lancelot). So Lancelot sets off on an endless series of quests, the real object of which is to put as much distance as possible between himself and the Queen. Unfortunately, the RAD type of person has such a profound sense of being incomplete in themselves that, if they can't be with the one they love, they find it all too easy to love the one they are with. One suspects, therefore, that Morgana Le Fey did not have to work too strong a magic in order to make Lancelot fall in love with Elaine of Astolat. When Mallory tells us that Morgana caused Lancelot to see Elaine *as if* she were Guinevere, he is describing the well known psychological process of *projection* in which the loved one is perceived not as themselves but as the lover wishes them to appear.

From this union, however, Galahad, the Grail-winner is born. Galahad is represented by the Rune EOLH, a Rune of sacrifice. Nor surprisingly, having achieved the Grail, Galahad elects to remain in eternal glory, forsaking for ever the world of mundane pleasures. The Grail itself is represented by WYNN, since the happiness denoted by this Rune will always suggest something different to each of us, just as the Grail appears to have a different significance (and even a different physical appearance) for each of the Grail-winners. Likewise, the finding of the Grail, the healing of the Fisher King and the blooming of the Wasteland in the Parsifal version of the story are represented by ING, the symbol of fertility. This legend also hides some of the more recondite secrets of male sexuality (the curing of the Fisher King's wound has a sexual significance) which is also appropriate to ING, whose character is a stylized representation of the male scrotum.

The plight of the Fisher King is epitomized by the Rune NIED, symbol of lack or dearth. And the Grail Quest, which is undertaken by all, but accomplished by few, is represented by YR. This Rune has much to do with the Sign of Sagittarius, just as RAD, Lancelot's Rune, has close associations with Gemini. Lancelot is the archetypal pattern of the Knight who seeks diligently for the Grail but is destined never to achieve it. Interestingly, it is a trait of both Gemini and Sagittarius to incline to the opinion that it is better to travel hopefully than to arrive.

The Lady Elaine, mother of the child Galahad, who prefers to remain demurely in her father's castle of Astolat than present herself at court in Camelot, is represented by BEORC, prime Rune of motherhood and domesticity.

Not all the Runes represent people, some of them stand for things. SIGEL, for instance, represents the Table Round. SIGEL is the Sun, who in his yearly journey passes through all the Sièges or seats of the celestial Round Table, which is at once the mirror of, and model for, its earthly counterpart. All the Sièges, too, are represented by Runes, but since it would occupy too much space to list them all, I will mention only the Siège Perilous, the place that could be filled only by the most perfect and holy knight in all Christendom. This Siège is represented by PEORTH, a passive Martian Rune, thus hinting that perfection and sanctity are to be attained through the manipulation and control of the inverted Mars force.

This intimation is further supported by the allocation of TIR to Arthur's magical sword Excalibur, and the Rune IS to Excalibur's equally magical scabbard. This scabbard was stolen by Arthur's half-sister Morgana Le Fey, whom we have already met in the story of Lancelot and Elaine. Morgana is represented by the Rune HAGALL, and there are obvious connections between hail and ice. Moreover, HAGALL is an ambivalent Rune, sometimes fortunate and at other times the reverse. This well describes the character of Morgana, who is by no means a totally evil force in Arthurian tradition. She is often disruptive, but the knights and ladies of the court are apt to become a shade too complacent if they are not shaken out of their lethargy from time to time. This is especially true during the period subsequent to Arthur's final subjugation of Britain, which he accomplishes quite early on in his reign.

The shining citadel of Camelot is represented by the Rune OTHEL, and exactly what this implies can best be grasped by meditation upon the Christian teachings on the New Jerusalem as set forth in the Book of Revelations, or on the Norse myth of the rebuilding of Middle Earth in the period immediately following Ragnarok.

Not only are the personalities connected with the Arthurian tradition depicted by the Runes, the precepts and morals of the chivalric code may also be discerned by the dedicated seeker. This is no more than one would expect, of course, since the Runes themselves are the repository of an almost parallel philosophy. The first three Runes in particular are associated with an important triad of teachings. FEOH represents the injunction to love one another, the highest consideration of the traditions of chivalry. UR personifies the law of change and implies that nothing lasts for ever; or as Tennison says in his *Idylls of the King*, 'the old order changeth yielding place to new'. The Rune THORN is a reminder that, no matter what evils beset him, the knight should not become dispirited, at all times putting his faith in God (or in runic terms, the Universal Forces).

JARA, representing reward and punishment, is the symbol of the Law of Karma, particularly that aspect of it which, way back in the trendy sixties, was popularly referred to as Instant Karma. It is an effect most clearly to be seen at work in the story of *Gawain and the Green Knight*, where, towards the end of the narrative, Gawain receives a cut on his neck from the axe of the Green Knight because he has failed to keep an oath which requires him to yield up in the evening everything that has come into his possession during the day.

Finally, there are the two Runes MANN and EOH to be considered. MANN, with its emphasis on interdependence, represents the finer ideals of chivalry, as well as embodying the philosophy that what is done for one is done for all. EOH, however, may be looked at on two levels. On the first, this Rune represents the faithful horse, without which a knight would not be a knight (the very word 'chivalry' comes from the French word for a horse *cheval*). On the second, EOH is a reminder that it is not only mankind which is interconnected on the subtle planes; humanity is also linked to every other species on the planet, all of us being, as it were, children of the same Mother.

These attributions are summed up in the following table:

Love one another

All things must pass

Faith in the Higher Powers

Merlin

Lancelot

Arthur

Guinevere

The Grail

Morgana le Fey

The Fisher King

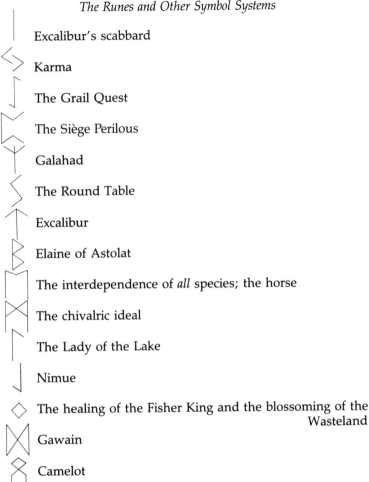

Excalibur's scabbard

Karma

The Grail Quest

The Siège Perilous

Galahad

The Round Table

Excalibur

Elaine of Astolat

The interdependence of *all* species; the horse

The chivalric ideal

The Lady of the Lake

Nimue

The healing of the Fisher King and the blossoming of the
                                                    Wasteland

Gawain

Camelot

The Runic System and the Qabalah

Perhaps the greatest syncretic system in the Western Esoteric Tradition is the Qabalah. Originally an exclusively Jewish preserve, the Qabalah has been adapted first to a Christian format and then, via the influence of the Christian Gnostics, into a sort of inter-denominational Gnosticism. Since the Hebrew Rabbis were at pains to demonstrate the omnipotence of their Deity over every aspect of life — the earth, the heavens and everything contained therein — they produced a philosophy which neatly explained (a) the interdependence of All, and (b) the upwelling of All from a single source. This is the same philosophy which underlies every mystical tradition, though it is consistently understated in myth and has never been so coherently explained (to the uninitiated at least) as it is in the Qabalistic exegesis. For instance: what Greek mythology calls Chaos (from a root meaning 'to gape'), Norse mythology calls

Ginnungagap, which likewise means a gaping hole, a yawning chasm; while in the Qabalistic system, the equivalent concept is called Negative Existence.

The main significance of the Qabalah is that it enables students to move from one tradition to another without seriously losing their way. It may be compared to Ariadne's thread, or to a magic key which can unlock the secrets of the mythological mode of thought. Such a tool is necessary to the student (or for that matter, the Adept) because it is important that one should not lose one's way when working in the Astral Light. To the unwary or the inexperienced, the Astral Light can be a treacherous realm. For those willing to undertake such a journey, however, much valuable information can be gleaned from the Astral Records concerning the Runes and how they affect the material world and the inner world of the human psyche.

The most commonly used method of accessing and exploring the Astral Light is called Pathworking. One might say that Pathworking is a type of meditation which relies for its effects on the use of the imaginative faculty. As opposed to some other forms of meditation technique which advise students to empty their minds, the aim of a Pathworking is to flood consciousness with selected symbolic images. It is thus a method of centering or delimiting one's sphere of attention which requires the minimum of effort as regards concentration. A Pathworking is usually a dramatized story which may be rooted in either history, myth or some other area of fiction. The student is asked to visualize themselves as participating in this drama, sometimes as an observer of events, at other times taking the part of one of the leading characters.

There are varying depths to Pathworkings, just as one's depth of absorption in a book or a television play may vary. If the subject matter is interesting enough, if one is seated or lying comfortably, if there are no outside distractions one may successfully 'lose' oneself in some narrative or drama. The same can be said of Pathworkings, with the added bonus that a transfer of consciousness may take place so that the physical body and physical reality in general are totally forgotten and, for the duration of the working, the Astral Light becomes the only 'real' world the student knows. That is to say: the participant experiences a waking dream, a dream which, unlike normal dreams, allows him (or her) complete control in matters of judgement, discrimination and memory.

This, however, is the deepest level of Pathworking. Novices invariably remain aware of their physical bodies, extraneous noises and the fact that they are only 'seeing pictures in their heads' for some considerable time before they experience this 'shift of levels'. Then they may begin to experience brief changes in consciousness during a working, though at first they will be unable to extend or regulate these changes by their own volition. These shifts of consciousness gradually grow more frequent and their duration longer until, finally, a transfer of awareness will occur near the beginning of a session and continue until it is over.

Many students get quite upset, even indignant, when a shift of levels fails to occur at their second or third attempt. In my experience, however, those people who are naturally clairaudient or clairsentient rather than clairvoyant do not experience a transfer of consciousness on a visual level on anything like a regular basis. Their talents lie in different directions and consequently their shifts take place in other areas of consciousness entirely. The effectiveness, and if you like, the reality of these shifts of consciousness can be assessed by the length of time it takes such people to return to a 'normal', everyday state of mind following participation in a Pathworking. Evidently, a meditation of this kind may be 'deep' without producing a shift of visual consciousness.

Which brings me to my next point. The question every novice asks is: Are Pathworkings safe? And the answer is that Pathworkings are as safe as driving a car. You won't come to any harm as long as you follow the rules. So what are these rules?

1. As far as possible, you should use a 'door' to get yourself onto the Astral Light, and also return by one. These 'doors' are usually visualized as exactly that: a door or archway leading to another world. But there is another meaning ascribed by occultists to the word *door*. Almost any magical symbol can be used as a 'door', and the part of the Astral Light to which one is admitted will differ according to the symbol employed. In the two Pathworkings which follow, I have combined both these meanings so that one finds oneself faced with a conventional doorway to which is affixed a runic symbol. After a while the door opens and a landscape is revealed, a landscape pertinent to that particular symbol. In the second Pathworking, I have not used a door in order to return to everyday consciousness but have employed an alternative method in which a semblance of dreaming is produced so that the astral traveller does not so much 'return' as 'awaken'. However, if you wish to go exploring any other runic pathways on your own account, I would advise you to stick to the more usual 'door' method.

2. Until you know your way around the Astral Light, use a 'mind map' such as the Qabalistic Tree of Life shown in Figure 36. In order to get some idea of what awaits you on each of these Paths, or at the various 'stations' or junction points (represented as circles on the diagram), you would be advised to read *The Shining Paths* by Dolores Ashcroft Nowicki (Aquarian Press, 1983). While for the more daring, I would recommend careful study of J.H. Brennan's *Astral Doorways* (Aquarian Press, 1980).

3. Always start out from a section of the Astral Light with which you are familiar. Try, also, to finish in an area you already know. Sometimes this will mean returning to a previous point on the Path, even on occasion to your original starting point. The two runic Pathworkings that follow will supply you with two initial departure points from which you may branch out, and by assiduously tracing out each Path, you will eventually be able to cover the entire Tree.

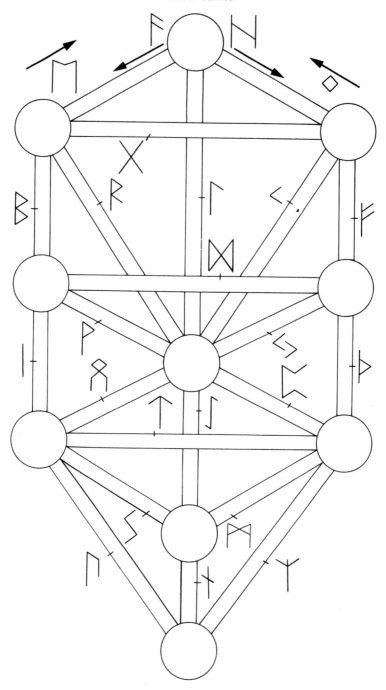

Figure 36: The Runes on the Qabalistic Tree of Life

4.   Where possible, allow yourself to be shown around by a Guide. This is not always an option open to you, but where it is, I urge you to take it. However, not all figures who present themselves as Guides are friendly, though they are more likely to be mischievous in character than downright malevolent. The denizens of the Astral Light constitute another order of being with a different set of ethics, values and priorities from those that humankind are used to. Therefore, each Guide should be questioned or tested before you agree to accompany them. On a runic Pathworking, a simple but effective test is to draw with your forefinger the shape of the Rune which equates to the Path you are on (the one you have used as a 'door' onto the Astral) between yourself and the putative Guide. Usually, this symbol will glow so that the runic letter can be seen quite clearly. At this point a 'false Guide' will either vanish or literally be revealed in his or her true colours. A genuine Guide will make an answering gesture, either repeating your original symbol or drawing the *Triangle of Fate*, the downward pointing triangle used to gain access to the Guardians of Runic Knowledge as demonstrated in the first Pathworking given below.

5.   If in doubt — if, for instance, you are faced with a threatening figure or find yourself being offered an object of which you are suspicious — retrace your steps to an area of the Astral that you know and return to normal consciousness. By far and away the greatest number of menacing presences encountered on the Astral Light are *Guardians* whose only duty is to block the way of those astral travellers who are ignorant of the correct Password (or Sign) that will allow them to pass by. These Guardians will not follow if you decide to retreat, nor will they in any way attempt to prevent you from doing so. Neither will a Guardian attack unless provoked. If you are unable to pass a Guardian, you will have to find a Guide who can tell you the Password (or show you the requisite Sign), or work them out yourself from first principles.

The Pathworkings
In order to make these imaginary journeys, I suggest that you first read through the relevant Pathworking and, if possible, record it on tape, making slight pauses where indicated, i.e. where a paragraph ends in three dots. If you do not possess a tape recorder, you will have to memorize the general outline of the Pathworking and repeat it back to yourself at the appropriate time. There is no need to learn the Pathworking word for word but all the salient incidents should be included and pauses made in the narration to give yourself time to look around.

   Choosing a time when you are unlikely to be disturbed, sit or lie in a comfortable position. It is better to be seated as there is then less danger of falling asleep during the session. Some students, however, get better results when lying down, so experiment until you discover which posture produces optimum results for you. Try to relax. The type of state you should aim for is one in which all *unnecessary* tension is eliminated while an air of expectancy and alertness is maintained. Now, switch on your tape recorder, or begin to tell yourself the 'story' of the Pathworking. Visualize the scenes and events of the working as clearly and as vividly as you are able.

And please take those last four words to heart. It is not necessary that you visualize so well that everything on the Astral appears as clear to you as when viewed with your physical eyes. This would be very nice but it is not *necessary*. All that is required is that you try as hard as you can. If your experiments in developing your intuition through divination have taught you that you work better through one of your other psychic senses, then be prepared to find yourself employing that sense also while on your astral travels. (Being more clairsentient than clairvoyant, I do not, myself, possess a marked degree of natural skill in visualization.)

At the end of a Pathworking session it is advisable to stand up and walk about as soon as you are able, and to have something to eat and drink, even if it is only a biscuit and a hot drink. These activities ensure the rapid return of one's thought processes to the level of physical being. This occurs because there is an aspect of consciousness which is responsible for the motor activity of the body and for regulating the mechanism of digestion, and there is no better method of 'earthing' than walking and eating. You should also make a note of the most important impressions gained or any strong responses to events witnessed on the Astral Light. Such records can be very revealing when examined in retrospect as impressions or realizations which succeed in stamping themselves on consciousness are generally cumulative in effect, one 'revelation' building on previous realizations.

The first Pathworking, The Way to the Norns, is intended to re-awaken any Teutonic, Norse or early Anglo-Saxon memories lying dormant in the personal unconscious and should be performed by any serious runic shaman *before* moving on to the more Qabalistic type of Pathworking. Indeed, some students may find that the repeated travelling of this Path will lead them to the nine 'Worlds' of Nordic cosmogony: Midgard, our starting point, Asgard, Alfheim, Jotonheim, Vanaheim, Svartalfheim, Helheim, Muspellsheim and Niflheim.

The second example is an illustration of a Qabalistic Pathworking. Figure 36 is a drawing of the Qabalistic Tree of Life with the Runes of the Elder Futhark set out on the twenty-two Paths. As you can see, two of the Paths have been allocated two Runes each, one for ascending the relevant Path and the other for descending.

The Way to the Norns

Imagine before you a wooden door with an arched top. Inlaid into the door is a silver downward-pointing triangle. There is no handle or keyhole on this side of the door, for this door can only be opened from within. Visualize the door and its symbol as vividly and intently as you are able. Be willing to watch and wait until something happens . . .

Slowly the door swings outwards onto a sunlit scene. Before you on a low mound is an ancient and gnarled tree in full leaf. To one side is a dense, dark wood, eerily silent, to the other side is a bridge of ice stretching from a point near the grassy mound up to the snow-topped mountains in the near distance.

In imagination you rise from your seat and pass through the doorway into the sunlit world beyond.

The air is warm in this new world and at once sweet and acrid with woodland smells. The ice bridge shimmers with rainbow colours in the gentle sunlight. The tree before you is immensely tall and a soft breeze shakes its large leaves intermittently so that they rustle like the whispering of a hundred voices. As you stand gazing up at the tree, a little procession begins to wend its way up from below the far side of the mound on which the tree stands. This procession consists of three female figures. Leading is a young girl of about eleven or twelve with loose ash-blonde hair. Following her is a matronly-looking woman with flaxen hair plaited into two swag plaits which hang down to her breasts. Last of all comes an older woman with grey hair coiled neatly about her head. All three wear long, loose robes and carry a pitcher or vase before them. Slowly they circle the mound, gradually moving inwards towards the bole of the tree . . .

When at last they are standing among the roots of the giant tree, they pour out their libations of pure, clear water onto the ground. Then after a brief pause, they begin to return the way they came, the young girl still in the lead.

You follow them at a discreet distance to the far side of the mound, where you discover a tunnel entrance, rather like a huge rabbit-hole, leading under the roots of the tree. The procession enters this tunnel and after hesitating for a moment, unsure what you should do, you enter also. In the tunnel it is neither dark nor bright but a kind of twilight, though you can see your way well enough. A path leads straight ahead, tending downwards at an easy angle. Before you, you can see the retreating figure of the grey-haired woman who brings up the rear of the little procession. You set off down the tunnel, aware that you are entering a different level, a different state of consciousness; a place that is not a place, where the rules of life are at once both more simple and more primitive than those of the world you have left behind; a place of paradox, where there are no barriers between true and false, fast and slow, near and far . . .

The tunnel is very long and, no matter how fast you walk, you cannot seem to catch up with the three women ahead of you. Suddenly you are aware that you are alone in the tunnel, and you feel a small pang of unease as you realize that you are without a guide in an alien environment. Almost at once, however, you see in the distance a faint bluish light which indicates that you are nearing the end of your journey. The light grows larger and you can see that the tunnel gives out onto a huge cavern, most of which is filled with an underground lake. You enter the cavern and look around you. In the centre of the lake, far off, is a tiny island. To your left stand the three female figures, now without their pitchers, looking severe. The woman with the flaxen plaits comes forward and demands to know what you are doing here. She tells you that no one may enter the sacred precinct merely in order to satisfy their idle curiosity.

You reply that you have come with the intention of reawakening the runic memories slumbering deep in your own unconscious and in the unconscious of the race; you vow that you will use those memories, if you should be vouchsafed them, for the benefit and advancement of all living things.

Your interrogater looks over her shoulder to where the older female stands waiting, and there is a glint in the eyes of the older woman as she solemnly nods her grey head in silent assent to the other's unspoken question. The woman with the flaxen plaits tells you that her sister is willing for you to drink from the Well of Memory but that on this occasion you are not to speak to either the older woman or the young girl, for their wisdom is for another time.

Now the older woman leads you round the edge of the underground lake to a slit-like opening in the rock. Through this opening you can see another cavern and, within it, another lake. You can also hear the gush and gurgle of a small waterfall somewhere in the distance. The older woman passes through into the second cave and then looks back as if to urge you on.

Her eyes are kindly and knowing as if she understood and forgave all your past failings and mistakes, all your weaknesses and backslidings. There is much you would like to ask her, but she raises a finger to her lips in warning and you pass through the opening in the rocks with your thoughts unspoken.

This second cavern is light and airy, and the lake here is not as large as the one you have just left. The waters of this lake are pure and clear; so clear that you can see right down to the bottom of the lake and make out coloured pebbles and even grains of sand lying there. A low waterfall, less than a metre high and perhaps three metres in width, pours into the lake, issuing from a mysterious and inky blackness towards the rear of the cave.

To your right, in a niche just above the waterline, is a metal cup fixed to the rock by an iron chain. On a ledge overlooking the whole scene as if it were the symbolic guardian of the place, is an idol in the form of a bearded head set on an upright stake. This idol is so lifelike that, apart from the fact that the eyes are closed, it could almost be a real human head watching over the sacred waters, protecting them from violation by the profane.

The older woman dips the metal cup into the waters of the Well of Memory and offers it to you. Taking the cup from her, you place it to your lips and drink. The water is very cold but not unpleasant, reminding you of all the tastes you like best in the world . . .

You pass the cup back to its keeper and she replaces it carefully on its shelf. Then she leads you slowly back to the first cavern where her sisters are waiting silently for your return. You bow in thanks to the older woman but you remember the warning given you by the second sister and are careful not to speak . . .

Then the middle sister herself comes forward and explains that on future visits you will be free to roam these caves at will, though, she warns, you would be wise to wait at the entrance to the first cavern for one of the sisters to appear to act as your guide. There are, she says, dwarves and trolls in the further caves, not all of them amicably disposed to human kind. With these words she leads you to the mouth of the long, straight tunnel leading back to the realm of Middle Earth and sets you on your way.

As you walk this path you become more and more certain that you have visited the first lake and its barren island before. Even the tunnel you are in at this moment seems vaguely familiar to you. You rack your memory, trying to remember where and when . . .

The journey upwards seems to take you far less time than the journey down and quite soon you find yourself emerging from the tunnel between the roots of the ancient tree and entering the warm sunlight. The dark wood stands to one side of you and the bridge of ice to the other. But these paths are for another day, perhaps . . .

For the present, you are ready to return, so you walk around the grassy mound on which the great tree stands and look for the door by which you entered this strange world, the door without a key. It is there waiting for you, still open. And through the doorway you can see the room you left behind. You can see your physical body, eyes closed and at rest, waiting to be re-inhabited.

You pass through the door and it closes silently behind you. You hear the sound as of a key being turned in a lock and you return to your physical body . . . Gently, very gently, awareness of your bodily sensations begins to return and, in your own time, you acclimatize yourself to being back in the world of material reality . . . Gently, very gently, you return to the physical world of everyday events feeling refreshed and happy. In your own time, you come back to normal consciousness feeling relaxed and contented, contented and relaxed.

Exploring the Astral

Once you have made this journey and drunk from the Well of Memory, you will begin to gain certain insights into the runic system which had previously evaded you. These insights will occur during incidents in your everyday life. They will not occur in dreams or while you are out on the Astral. In fact, they generally take the form of a bright idea which comes in an instant yet is often incredibly complex both in its form and ramifications.

After the first journey, you may dispense with the tape recorder and pass through the doorway to visit the field where the ancient tree stands whenever you wish. If you choose to go down the tunnel, you will usually find one or other of the Three Norns waiting for you. Sometimes all three will be present though generally only one of them will assume the role of Guide at any one time. If none of the sisters are waiting, DO NOT GO ON until one of them comes for you. If they do not appear, go back; they have nothing to show you that day. So long as one of the Norns is with you, you are safe. Even if you should come across the dragon Nidhogg who lives near the deepest root of the tree, the Norns will protect you.

Some students prefer to explore the terrain surrounding the tree itself. This is perfectly permissible, but be reconciled to the fact that you may not get very far. The bridge has a Guardian who never sleeps and whose hearing is so acute that he can detect the footfalls of a cat. This Guardian will bar your way, though if you can discover the password, he will become your Guide and lead you to one of the glittering palaces which lie on the further side of the rainbow bridge.

The dark wood is protected by wild animals, mostly wolves and bears, but sometimes smaller creatures such as otters or badgers put in an appearance. It is not a good idea to set foot in this wood without a reliable Guide. The Norns make good Guides on this part of the Astral, especially the eldest, but can rarely be inveigled into entering the Iron Wood. Some of the animals, too, will act as Guides if you can induce them to take human form. In animal form they are not to be trusted. (This only applies to animals in the Iron Wood; elsewhere on the Astral, animals usually make trustworthy and efficient way-showers.)

If any of the foregoing information puts you off the idea of Pathworking, stick to underground travels with the Norns or wander around the vast plain that stands before the tree and see who you meet there. Or move on to the Qabalistic Pathworkings which are safer though 'tamer'. Here is an example of the kind of conditions you can expect to encounter on a Qabalistic Pathworking.

The Path of Nied

Before you in your imagination there emerges a tall oak door with a circular bronze handle. Inlaid into the door at about eye level is the Rune NIED also in bronze. Hold this picture in your mind's eye as clearly and as strongly as you can.

As you watch, the door swings open outwards revealing a pearl-grey mist beyond. Still in imagination, you rise from your seat and approach the doorway. Though the mist, a low moorland landscape can be discerned, and at your feet is a broad path or trackway wide enough for several people to walk abreast. You step onto this trackway and start to walk along it. Almost immediately, the mist clears and you find yourself on a serpentine path which winds its way across the wild moors, finally terminating in a large stone circle on the horizon. This stone circle is formed of natural, undressed standing stones, little more than large boulders, which have an air of raw and primitive vitality about them that can be sensed even at a distance.

The dawn sky is cloudy and the day has not yet fully begun. A chill wind touches your face, but something about the moor and the stone circle expresses a welcome as if they expected you, as if you were a traveller returning after many years to a place you had once known well. Indeed, looking down at yourself you find that you are dressed in a grey woollen traveller's cloak and that in your right hand you carry a pilgrim's staff.

Moving swiftly along the twisting path, you come to the point where it enters the stone circle passing between two pitted, grey-brown menhirs. These ancient sentinels hold no terrors for you and you pass between them happily, almost gaily.

In the centre of the circle is a small fire made of twigs. On approaching the fire, you see that the twirl-stick and bow which have been used to light it have been carefully laid to one side. Obviously someone has recently lit this fire and cannot be far away. You look around hoping to catch sight of a fellow traveller who may act as a companion or even a guide. But there is no one to be seen.

The sun has risen now and everything around you has become more colourful and interesting. The boulders are browner and the grass greener. There are birds calling and flying overhead, sweeping and wheeling from one side of the sky to the other.

On the far side of the stone circle you can now see that another pathway, serpentine like the first, continues on over the moors, meandering out of sight between two low hills.

Since there is nothing to detain you in the circle, you move onto this pathway and follow it down into a little hollow. . . Here you find a narrow stream of swiftly flowing water spanned by a white stone bridge. Beyond the bridge, half hidden by some trees, is a long, low building also of white stone with a thatched roof. At one end of this structure is a pair of double doors, one of which stands invitingly ajar.

Eagerly, feeling that you have reached your destination at last, you cross the little bridge and approach the entrance. The interior of the building looks dark and is redolent with the scent of sweet woods being burnt. Coming from the back of the building, or perhaps from behind it, is the sound of soft humming or chanting so low that you are unable to make out either the tune or the words with any certainty.

You enter the darkness and stand still for a moment waiting for your eyes to adjust to the lack of light. Towards the centre of the building you can just make out a huge cauldron, steaming over a log fire, and at the back of the building, beyond the cauldron, is a life-sized statue of a man. Round his head is a silver fillet and his body is swathed in a heavy purple cloak decorated with a gold fringe. Through the steam of the cauldron this figure seems to beckon you to approach.

You step forward and are at once enveloped in a white-and-silver mist shot through here and there with a rainbow iridescences. Within this mist you can see scenes of your childhood, scenes from nature: animals, insects, representations of the seasons and the elements . . .

Then, slowly, the mist clears and you are once more seated in your chair in your own familiar room.

On retreading this Path you will probably come across the figure who lit the need-fire, for he is hidden somewhere among the images presented to you. This person will act as your Guide while you are on the Path of Nied but will eventually hand you over to the 'living statue' from the white stone building, or to one of this statue's representatives. However, it is not so imperative to have a Guide when following the Qabalistic Paths and much can be discovered in this system by solo reconnoitres.

Divination Practice
The Life Chart

Except that it uses all twenty-five Runes, this runecast is very like the Astrological runecast given on page 125.

Lay the Runes face down on your diviner's cloth. Swirl and set them out in the order shown in Figure 37. This layout can be used in exactly the same way as the previous Astrological runecast, to give more detailed information concerning the events of the coming year. However, it is more frequently used as a Life Chart, showing the broad outline of the querent's destiny in regard to all twelve divisions of life.

The House in which WYRD falls often signifies the area of life experience through which the querent can expect to be rewarded (or punished) for their

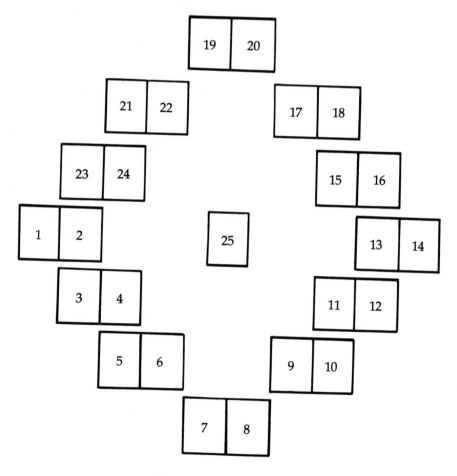

Figure 37: The Life Chart

previous actions,* or it may indicate what lessons the querent is supposed to be assimilating in the present life. Note carefully, therefore, in which House the Blank Rune is situated and with which Rune it is paired. This will indicate the area in which the querent has the greatest capacity for success or failure, depending on whether the Rune with which WYRD is associated possesses a positive or a negative connotation.

The central Rune signifies that feature of the querent's personality which most impresses itself on the outside world, for good or ill.

This is not an easy runecast to interpret, nor is it one which will appeal to everyone. One can do more harm than good through a mistaken interpretation of a Life Chart than with any other runecast, so practise it thoroughly before trying it out on your family and friends. And if you don't feel in tune with this runecast, then for Odin's sake leave it alone — it is obviously not for you.

If you do attempt a life reading, however, do not condemn your querent to a lifetime of unredeemed misery. Remember that the Runes will always offer some indication as to how negative influences may be combated.

---

* If you do not believe in reincarnation, you should assume that these actions have been committed earlier in the present life. Whatever your beliefs, however, I should point out that this runecast deals *solely* with the *results* of previous actions and not with the revelation of those actions — though, with experience, your own heightened intuitive faculties may provide you with some interesting insights into that side of things.

Chapter 12
WHAT COMES NEXT?

There is enough information in the previous chapters to keep the average student occupied for some considerable time. In the sphere of divination the main key to success is practice, practice and yet more practice. But if you wish to develop your skills as a runic magician, you will need to get on better terms with the gods and goddesses of the Northern pantheon. First, you will need to discover the names and attributions of these deities. Secondly, you will have to experience the Norse/Teutonic archetypes as psychological realities. This is best done by meditating on each deity in turn, or by undertaking a series of Pathworkings that will bring you face to face with the various god-forms of the Northern tradition. Unfortunately, to perform a Pathworking without also possessing the necessary background information is not likely to lead to any significant progress being made. Students following this course of action are apt to come up against potencies they do not understand and to find their way barred by the Astral Guardians at an early stage in their explorations. The passwords by which one gains access to the Nine Worlds and the majestic palaces of Asgard are intimately connected with the attributes and characteristics of the spiritual beings who have their homes there. To confuse matters even further, these 'passwords' need not be words at all. They can be signs or symbols, or even a state of mind. Thus, the ecologically-minded are able to enter Alfheim, the abode of the Bright Elves, as if by right, while those who have no feeling for the Earth and growing things will find access to this part of the Astral virtually impossible.

In this book, I have kept references to Norse and Teutonic mythology to a minimum since a detailed discussion of this subject would have tended to confuse the main object under investigation — the Runes. There are many good books about the Northern deities and a selection of these are listed in the Bibliography. The trouble with most books on mythology is that they are written by academics who lack a magical background. Hence the whole emphasis of these works seems lop-sided from an esoteric point of view. Also, in the same way that there are glaring differences between the Greek and

Roman systems, despite their initial homogeneous appearance, so there are wide differences between the Teutonic, Norse and Anglo-Saxon myths and deities. In fact these three cultures represent three separate though related Paths, the Norse being the one most commonly followed. The Anglo-Saxon Path is the most obscure because so much information relating to it seems to have gone astray. However, the work of Dr Brian Bates is doing much to reclaim and reinstate the ancient and hitherto neglected heritage of the English speaking peoples, and hopefully this trend will continue.

Some students may prefer to further their studies in association with a group or under the auspices of a qualified Runemaster (or mistress). There are several groups working with the Runes, and Edred Thorsson in his book *Futhark: a Handbook of Rune Magic* mentions some British and American contacts. Other groups occasionally advertise vacancies in the occult press but one must keep a sharp eye out for these as such gaps are quickly filled and the advertisements rarely repeated. If, however, there are no runic study groups operating in your area, you can always start your own with the co-operation of a few like-minded friends. Much can be achieved, even working alone, through dedication and sincerity.

On the other hand, the runic Path is intrinsically a solitary one. Do not be surprised, therefore, if you are expected to make progress without the benefit of human companionship. If such a situation arises, view it positively. The fellowship of the Northern gods and goddesses, the Elves and the Dwarves will more than recompense you for the lack of human comrades. And if you remain convinced that the only way you will ever progress is through personal tuition at the hands of a runic shaman, then bear in mind the Eastern proverb, 'When the pupil is ready the master cometh', and strive with every fibre of your being to get yourself into that state of readiness. Then when your teacher finally appears you will be in a position to recognize your opportunity and to make the most of it.

Runic wisdom is more easily available in the world today in the form of books, articles, lectures and study groups than it has been for the previous nine centuries. Read, study, practise runic divination and magic, and the next piece of information, the next step along the Path will be revealed to you at the right time and in the right way. The most important lesson you will ever learn is that the Universal Forces are to be trusted, that where necessary they themselves will instruct and lead the aspiring student. Or as my Teacher used to tell me: Be prepared to discover that the Cosmos is friendly.

INDEX